Social Issues in Literature

Women's Issues in Alice Walker's *The Color Purple*

Other Books in the Social Issues in Literature Series:

Censorship in Ray Bradbury's *Fahrenheit 451*

Gender in Lorraine Hansberry's *A Raisin in the Sun*

Genocide in *The Diary of Anne Frank*

Tyranny in William Shakespeare's *Julius Caesar*

War in John Knowles's *A Separate Peace*

War in Tim O'Brien's *The Things They Carried*

Women's Search for Independence in Charlotte Brontë's *Jane Eyre*

Social Issues
in Literature

Women's Issues in Alice Walker's *The Color Purple*

Claudia Durst Johnson, Book Editor

GREENHAVEN PRESS
A part of Gale, Cengage Learning

GALE
CENGAGE Learning

Detroit • New York • San Francisco • New Haven, Conn • Waterville, Maine • London

Christine Nasso, *Publisher*
Elizabeth Des Chenes, *Managing Editor*

© 2011 Greenhaven Press, a part of Gale, Cengage Learning

Gale and Greenhaven Press are registered trademarks used herein under license.

For more information, contact:
Greenhaven Press
27500 Drake Rd.
Farmington Hills, MI 48331-3535
Or you can visit our Internet site at gale.cengage.com

For product information and technology assistance, contact us at

Gale Customer Support, 1-800-877-4253
For permission to use material from this text or product, submit all requests online at www.cengage.com/permissions

Further permissions questions can be emailed to permissionrequest@cengage.com

Articles in Greenhaven Press anthologies are often edited for length to meet page requirements. In addition, original titles of these works are changed to clearly present the main thesis and to explicitly indicate the author's opinion. Every effort is made to ensure that Greenhaven Press accurately reflects the original intent of the authors. Every effort has been made to trace the owners of copyrighted material.

Cover photograph copyright © Bettmann/Corbis.

LIBRARY OF CONGRESS CATALOGING-IN-PUBLICATION DATA

Women's issues in Alice Walker's The color purple / Claudia Durst Johnson, book editor.
        p. cm. -- (Social issues in literature)
    Includes bibliographical references and index.
    ISBN 978-0-7377-5270-0 -- ISBN 978-0-7377-5271-7 (pbk.)
    1. Walker, Alice, 1944- Color purple--Juvenile literature. 2. African American women in literature--Juvenile literature. I. Johnson, Claudia Durst, 1938-
    PS3503.R167F334 2011
    813'.54--dc22

                                                    2010034624

Printed in the United States of America
   2 3 4 5 6   15 14 13 12 11

FD189

Contents

Introduction   9

Chronology   12

Chapter 1: Background on Alice Walker

1. Walker's Childhood, Education, and Crusade   16
   for African American Women
   Barbara T. Christian

   Walker was active in the civil rights movement and pioneered the study of the relationship between black men and women.

2. Alice Walker's Childhood Sense of Betrayal   24
   Evelyn C. White

   Alice Walker's blinding in one eye and disfigurement when she was eight years old left her traumatized for life.

3. Feeling Like an Outsider   31
   Maria Lauret

   Walker appreciated a sense of community in her childhood but has seen herself as an outsider, whether it is in her family or among her literary peers.

Chapter 2: *The Color Purple* and Women's Issues

1. From Being Dominated to Taking Charge   39
   Donna Haisty Winchell

   The Color Purple paints a picture of a cruel, male-dominated society that leads Celie to lose her love for men and create a reversal in gender roles.

2. Being Deprived of a Mother's Bond   50
   Charles L. Proudfit

   Celie's damaging relationship with her mentally ill mother sets her in search of other female bonds.

3. The Myth of the Rape and Silencing of   58
   Philomela Informs *The Color Purple*
   Martha J. Cutter

Like the mythical Philomela, Celie is raped and silenced, but her symbolic connections with blood and birds lead her, unlike Philomela, to creativity and freedom.

4. Walker Revises Traditional Gender Roles   **65**
   Mae G. Henderson

   In a culture of male cruelty, women sacrifice for one another and replace traditional marriage with an extended family.

5. Trading Male Literary Traditions for Female   **74**
   Oral Ones
   Valerie Babb

   The black woman's oral tradition (in which the novel is written) supersedes the white male's written one.

6. Walker's Relationship with the African   **81**
   American Male
   Philip M. Royster

   The male audiences of Walker's novel and the film made from the novel were vocal and outraged at the picture she drew of black men as cruel and heartless.

7. Folk Art as a Means to Female Survival   **89**
   Keith E. Byerman

   In *The Color Purple* women use folk wisdom to overcome their male oppressors. Folk art, including sewing and singing, makes it possible for them to survive, have their revenge, and tell about their pain.

8. Male Cruelty Leads to Positive Changes   **98**
   Henry O. Dixon

   Male cruelty in *The Color Purple* leads to positive development in the lives of female characters.

9. Centering on Women but Ignoring Race   **108**
   and Economics
   bell hooks

   The novel, while attacking the exploitation of females in an African American community, fails to challenge the whole system of racial and class exploitation.

10. *The Color Purple* Is a Disservice   **113**
    to Black Women
    Trudier Harris

In taking an independent view of the novel, one finds an unbelievably subservient, uncomplaining protagonist and white stereotypes of black men and women.

Chapter 3: Contemporary Perspectives on Women's Issues

1. Women Achieve Social Change Through Folk Art   **125**
    Anne Constable

Around the world, women find economic and social power through cooperation and the revival of traditional art in a misogynistic society.

2. Domestic Violence Retains Cultural   **130**
    Momentum Worldwide
    Sonya Weakley

One in three women is abused worldwide. Abuse of women is so ingrained in cultures that victims will rarely testify in court about the abuse.

3. Conflicting Feminist Ideologies Among   **134**
    Black Women
    Patricia Hill Collins

The black women who recognize and want to work for the betterment of their sisters are hampered by their conflicting ideologies.

4. A Black Celebrity Decides to Make Her   **141**
    Sexual Orientation Known
    Ari Karpel

After Wanda Sykes told the public that she is a lesbian, she became a spokesperson for black and gay America.

For Further Discussion   **151**

For Further Reading   **152**

Bibliography   **153**

Index   **158**

Introduction

In 1985 just before the opening of the film *The Color Purple*, based on Alice Walker's novel, with an all-star cast including Oprah Winfrey and Whoopi Goldberg, a coalition was formed to boycott the film across the country. Beginning with its premiere in Los Angeles, theaters showing the film were met with picket lines and general protests as African American men walked back and forth in front of theaters carrying signs objecting to both the film and the novel.

Many literary critics have, throughout the years, either ignored the novel or attacked it for its characterizations, themes, and language. Yet it won a 1983 Pulitzer Prize—the first ever awarded to an African American woman—the 1983 American Book Award, and a nomination for a 1982 National Book Critics Circle Award. While critics of the novel have objected to the stereotyping of black women in the novel, the demonizing of black men, and the fairy-tale ending in a story that largely ignores race, defenders of the novel have argued that African Americans' preoccupation with defense against whites has caused them to be blind to sexual abuse within their own communities.

The discord over *The Color Purple* derives from two histories of subjugation that have become entangled and frequently work against one another. The most prominent issue in the novel is the physical and psychological abuse of women in the age-old traditional patriarchy. This subjugation has been suffered in varying degrees by white and black women alike. Its basis in the United States was religious. Throughout the nation in the nineteenth and early twentieth centuries, it was preached from powerful and influential pulpits that women deserved the ill treatment they received because Eve had been tempted by the devil to disobey God, had tempted Adam to do the same, and as a result had caused them to be thrown out of the Garden of Eden, cursing mankind forever.

In 1860 the prominent clergyman John Angell James wrote in *Female Piety* that "woman was the cause of sin and death in our world." Moreover, women were weak minded, irresponsible, unreliable, untrustworthy, and immoral, he contended. Therefore, it was the responsibility of fathers, brothers, and husbands to keep women from doing further damage by keeping them under strict control and out of the public arenas, where they might try to compete with men for power. This philosophy permitted, and even encouraged, physical abuse of women. Women in many households became the targets of rage—the "whipping boys"—when men suffered. Men were unable to vent their rage over grievances against those who had power over them, so they "took it out" on the women over whom they did have control. Frequently, as is suggested by the alliance between the women's movement and the temperance movement in the nineteenth century, the violence was triggered by alcohol, which many men used as a means of escape. Into the early decades of the twentieth century, during which *The Color Purple* is set, wife-beating was an accepted practice of the culture, evidenced by state laws that "compassionately" limited the size of the stick with which violence could be applied.

In *The Color Purple*, what convolutes and renders the story of Celie, a battered woman, is that her abusers are African American men—members of another group of oppressed people. In Walker's novel the oppressed become the oppressors. One supposition is that because black men are unable to retaliate against the whites who cause their suffering, they, like many other men, take their fury out on those whom they can control—in this case, black women. Black women such as Celie suffer a double burden as a woman and an African American.

The history of the black woman in white society is an intricate one that has some bearing on Walker's novel, despite the charge that she ignores race altogether. As a slave, black women were beaten sadistically and raped by white men, forced to bear them children and then often separated from their children, as Celie is in *The Color Purple*. The roles of African American women were diverse, as they continue to be today. Even in times of slavery, reconstruction, and well into the twentieth century—even as badly treated as they were by whites—certain black women, especially domestics, had greater status than black men. They often had a real voice in the management of the households in which they worked. Black women ate their meals (segregated, of course) at the kitchen table, but black men were handed their meals through the back door to eat in the yard. African American women seemed more successful in starting up businesses, as Celie is able to do, as seamstresses, hair stylists, and caterers, for example. In any case, African American women increasingly became heads of their own households, drawing wages, providing for and disciplining their children as men could not do. This split in economic status and control within many households over the years likely created a breeding ground for gender animosity.

The following exploration of women's issues in *The Color Purple* is divided into three parts. First is the story of Alice Walker's poverty-stricken, isolated, and tragic childhood in a male-dominated community. Second is a group of critical readings from a variety of viewpoints relative to women's issues in *The Color Purple*. The issues addressed in the novel include rape; incest; physical and psychological abuse within families; dysfunctional families; love between women; stereotyping of black men and women; gender role reversal; the silencing of victimized women; the effect of female role models; the use of folk art such as sewing, quilting, and singing to free oppressed women; and the special nature of women's spiritual life. The final section is devoted to these issues as they arise in contemporary life.

Chronology

1824

In Mississippi, men lose the right to beat their wives.

1848

Women and their male supporters present grievances at the Seneca Falls Conference, asking for the right to control their own property, to receive an education, to be free to speak in public, and to vote.

1860

Women receive the right to their own wages in New York State.

1863

The Emancipation Proclamation frees slaves in rebel states.

1865

The Fifteenth Amendment gives male former slaves the right to vote.

The National Woman's Suffrage Association asserts its resentment that black men are given the vote while no women have suffrage.

1873

Bradwell v. Illinois refuses women the right to practice law or to engage in other professions or assume public positions.

1874

The North Carolina Supreme Court nullifies the right of a man to beat his wife.

1920

The Nineteenth Amendment gives women the right to vote.

1944
Alice Walker is born on February 9 in Eatonville, Georgia.

1952
Walker is shot by a BB gun while playing with her brothers and blinded in one eye.

1961–1963
Walker becomes involved with civil rights while attending Spelman College in Atlanta.

1964–1965
After a decade of struggle, civil rights are enacted, banning race and gender discrimination, particularly in hiring.

1965
Walker receives a bachelor of arts degree from Sarah Lawrence College in New York.

1965–1968
Walker continues her involvement in civil rights in Georgia, Mississippi, and New York City.

1967
She marries a white civil rights lawyer, Melvyn Roseman.

1967–
The women's liberation movement surges forward, urging equality with men.

1970
Walker publishes her first novel, *The Third Life of Grange Copeland*, beginning her career as an outstanding novelist, essayist, and poet.

1974–1975
Walker works as contributing editor for *Ms.* magazine.

1978
Walker moves to California, eventually establishing residences in Mendocino County and Berkeley.

1979
Minnesota passes the first law penalizing wife beaters.

1982
Walker publishes *The Color Purple*, her third novel.

1985
The film *The Color Purple* is released.

1989
Walker publishes her fourth novel, a feminist volume titled *The Temple of My Familiar*.

1992
The U.S. attorney general finds that spousal abuse is a leading cause of injuries to women aged fifteen to forty-four.

2004
Walker's *Now Is the Time to Open Your Heart* is published, and a musical production of *The Color Purple* premieres in Atlanta.

Background on
Alice Walker

Walker's Childhood, Education, and Crusade for African American Women

Barbara T. Christian

Barbara T. Christian was a faculty member at the University of California–Berkeley from 1971 until her death in 2000. She authored the groundbreaking work Black Women Novelists.

In this selection Christian asserts that behind Alice Walker's work lies the history of her ancestors in a time of slavery. Walker grew up in rural Georgia, the daughter of a sharecropper and the descendent of slaves. She is one of the first writers to explore frankly the relationship between black men and women, asserts Christian. Why, Walker asks, with all the cruel forces pressing on African Americans from white society, are they cruel to each other? From the time of her college years at Sarah Lawrence in New York, Walker began writing and working actively for civil rights for black people. Christian also describes how Walker began focusing more on the cruel treatment of black women by black men and formulating a black feminist movement, which she defined as "womanism."

Since 1968 when *Once*, her first work, was published, Alice Walker has sought to bring closer that day for which her maternal ancestors waited—"a day when the unknown thing that was in them would be known." In four collections of poetry, two volumes of short stories, three novels, and many essays, she has expressed with graceful and devastating clarity the relationship between the degree of freedom black women have within and without their communities and the "survival whole" of black people. Her particular angle of vision is sharpened by her use of the history of black people in this country, and therefore of the South, where they were most brutally enslaved. A Southerner, she also presents that land as the place from which their specific characteristics of survival and creativity have sprung. Her works confront the pain and struggle of black people's history, which for her has resulted in a deeply spiritual tradition. And in articulating that tradition, she has found that the creativity of black women, the extent to which they are permitted to exercise it, is a measure of the health of the entire society.

A writer who admits to "a rage to defy/the order of the stars/despite their pretty patterns," Walker consistently approaches the "forbidden" in society as a route to the truth. Perhaps the most controversial of her subjects is her insistence on investigating the relationships between black women and men, black parents and children, with unwavering honesty. A womanist (her term for a black feminist), Walker has, more than any contemporary writer in America, exposed the "twin afflictions" that beset black women, the sexism and racism that historically and presently restrict their lives. Walker develops literary forms (for example her concept of quilting, her use of folk language) that are based on the creative legacy left her by her ancestors. But that heritage is not only a source of her forms. Most important for Walker is its essence: that spirituality is the basis of the valuable and therefore of art. Unlike the stereotype of the socially conscious writer, she asserts "the importance of diving through politics and social forces to dig into the essential spirituality of individual persons." . . .

Walker's Upbringing

She was born 9 February 1944, the eighth and last child of Willie Lee and Minnie Lou Grant Walker, Eatonton, Georgia, sharecroppers. She grew up in that small Southern town at a time when many blacks, like her parents, worked in the fields for a pittance and when whites exerted control over practically every aspect of black life. Her childhood was filled with stories of past lynchings, and like other Southern black children she found "at 12 that the same little white girls who had been her playmates were suddenly to be called 'miss.'" The young Walker was certainly affected by the pervasiveness of the violent racist system of the South, especially the impact it had on black families. In an interview in *Library Journal* (15 June 1970) she explained how this relationship affected her first novel, *The Third Life of Grange Copeland* (1970): "I was curious to know why people in families (specifically black families) are often cruel to each other and how much of this cruelty is caused by outside forces such as various social injustices, segregation, unemployment, etc."

Perhaps Walker was particularly attuned to the relationship between social forces and personal development because at a young age she lived through the feeling of being an outcast. At eight she lost the sight of one eye when one of her older brothers shot her with a BB gun. Her eye was covered by a scar until she was fourteen, when a relatively simple operation corrected the disfigurement, which made her feel ugly; and for years she feared she would lose the sight of the other eye. This experience caused her really to notice relationships. For that reason, she also began to keep a notebook, in which she wrote poems, often in the fields, where she had some privacy. Her writings seem indelibly marked by these years, for she focuses sharply on relationships, not only between people but also between human beings and nature. And her sense of her difference probably contributed to her tendency to tread forbidden paths. Ironically, Walker was awarded a "rehabilitation scholarship" from Georgia, a state which systematically oppressed black people. That, along with the fact that she was valedictorian of her senior class, enabled her to go to Spelman College.

Although, to some extent, the child Walker felt separate, she was also a part of a community which nurtured her. In spite of the oppressiveness of the racist Southern system, she had many excellent teachers. They saved her from "feeling alone; from worrying that the world she was stretching to find might not exist." And they lent her books, for her a necessary element in her development: "Books became my world because the world I was in was very hard." Her community, as well as her teachers, knew the importance of education. The men of Eatonton built what the schools needed, and parents raised money to keep them going.

At an early age, Walker saw black people working together to accomplish goals necessary to their survival and development. Despite the limits imposed upon them, they felt responsible for each other. In one of her essays she recalls that growing up in the South, a black might be afraid of whites but not of blacks. As a little girl, she walked and played with black convicts who were accused of murder. This sense of "One Life" that black people share, their belief that they are a community with a functional history and culture is, for Walker, one reason for the persistence of struggle characteristic of black Southern tradition. It is not so much the grand sweep of history or the artifacts created as it is the relations of people to each other, young to old, parent to child, man to woman, that make up that heritage—a theme that Walker has treated persistently in her works. . . .

College Years

Walker left Eatonton to go to college, first at Spelman in Atlanta, then at Sarah Lawrence in New York. What she learned at these two very different institutions is indicative of her character and would influence her work. At that time Spelman was, in many ways, dedicated to turning Negro girls into ladies. However, during Walker's years there, the atmosphere of

Author Alice Walker, who examines the issues of race and gender in many of her works. AP Images/Wide World Photos.

the school was strongly affected by the civil rights movement, what Walker calls "the Southern Revolution." . . .

At Sarah Lawrence, she discovered, in her pregnancy, the aloneness of woman in her body, the extreme result of which could also be death. In this crisis, she was saved by other women who knew that they too could be in her place. And she recognized, as have so many other women, the different standards of acceptance for women and men within her own family as well as the outer society. Such recognition of the social definition of woman meant her experience was not just a private one—thus her public acknowledgment of her pregnancy and abortion as the impetus for her first published book, *Once*. Like other women in the 1970s, this and other peculiarly female experiences would result in Walker's recognition that she had to unite with other women to raise society's consciousness. As her first works of fiction, *The Third Life of Grange Copeland* (1970) and *In Love and Trouble* (1973), illustrate, Walker was one of the first contemporary black women writers to insist that sexism existed in the black community and was not only an issue for white women. She did this at a time when most black leaders focused only on racism and considered her position to be practically heresy. At the same time, she also dramatized in her works the nature of racism and the relationship between sexism and racism as modes of oppression that restricted the lives of all women and men in this country. Her experiences at Spelman and at Sarah Lawrence deepened her understanding of the interconnectedness of pivotal struggles for freedom in America. . . .

Critics' Disregard for Black *Women* Writers

In an interview in the early 1970s, Walker makes the connection between the fate of past Afro-American women writers and the attitudes that she herself had begun to encounter: "There are two reasons why the black woman writer is not taken as seriously as the black male writer. One is that she is a woman. Critics seem unusually ill-equipped to intelligently discuss and analyze the works of black women. Generally they do not even make the attempt; they prefer, rather, to talk about the lives of black women writers, not about what they write. And since black women writers are not, it would seem, very likeable (until recently they were the least willing worshippers of male supremacy) comments about them tend to be cruel." ...

Walker's third novel, *The Color Purple* (1982), exemplifies her belief that history is a necessary element of depth, that nothing is a product of the immediate present. Walker finished the novel after she and her husband divorced in 1977, and she moved to San Francisco. But she started writing it in New York City, where she tells us her major character, a rural early twentieth-century Southern black woman, seemed to elude her. It was not until she got a place in the country outside San Francisco that her characters' spirit, their language came rushing out. Whatever else critics may have said about this latest of Walker's works, they all agree that the black folk speech in which most of it is written is superb and resonates with a history of feeling and experience that is specifically Afro-American.

As is true of Walker's other two novels, this work spans generations of one poor black family in the context of rural Southern history. ...

Walker's Black Feminism Called Womanism

Walker's subject matter is also emphatically womanist, for the emphases in *The Color Purple* are on the oppression black women experience in their relationship with black men and the sisterhood they must share with each other in order to liberate themselves. As a vehicle for these themes, two sisters' letters—Celie's to God, Nettie's to Celie and finally Celie's to Nettie—provide the novel's form. Form and content, then, are inseparable.

Walker continues to explore "forbidden" sexual themes, as she did in *You Can't Keep A Good Woman Down*. In *The Color Purple* she focuses on incest in a black family and portrays a lesbian relationship as natural and freeing. And like many of the protagonists in her short stories, the heroines of her third novel triumph despite the tremendous odds against them. In an interview in *California Living*, Walker reveals that Celie was based on the story of her great-grandmother who at twelve was raped and abused. Yet though the story ends happily, Walker does not flinch from presenting the sexual abuse, the wife-beatings, and the violence that Celie undergoes in a society that demeans her as a woman. As in all of her works, violence is a result of the unnatural ideologies of sexism and racism. And though many readers and critics would prefer to ignore it, Walker has always insisted on exposing the violence inflicted upon black women's bodies and spirits.

In *The Color Purple* Walker adds another dimension to the sexism black women experience. Through Nettie, Celie's sister, who escapes her condition in the South to become a missionary, Walker describes the subordination of women to men in Africa. She therefore suggests that sexism for black women does not derive from racism, though it is qualitatively affected by it. "We're going to have to debunk the myth that Africa is a haven for black people—especially black women. We've been the mule of the world there and the mule of the world here."

Alice Walker's Childhood Sense of Betrayal

Evelyn C. White

An Afro-Canadian, Evelyn C. White is an author, journalist, and legal advocate for African American women. Her books include The Black Woman's Health Book *and* Chain, Chain, Change: For Black Women in Abusive Relationships.

The most traumatic episode in Alice Walker's life occurred when she was eight years old, according to White in this selection. While playing cowboys and Indians with BB guns their parents had given them, one of Walker's brothers shot her in the eye, causing a milky cataract, blinding her in one eye for life and causing an extensive scar. At the time, the boys urged her to lie about the incident. Alice's whole life turned upside-down, asserts White. Alice had been an outgoing, lively, "cute" child before the shooting. Afterward, even after surgery, the scars disfigured her. Schoolchildren ridiculed her, and she lost her sense of self-worth. Her grades dropped, White explains, and she became more and more withdrawn, turning to books for comfort. She also felt betrayed by members of her family: her brothers, who distorted the story, and her parents, who failed to take the "accident" seriously. Her brother declared years later that the family quickly got back to normal.

Injured in 1952, Alice would not offer a full account of the incident that cost her the vision in her right eye until the 1983 release of her essay, "Beauty: When the Other Dancer Is the Self." First published in *Ms.* magazine, the piece would later be included in her debut nonfiction collection, *In Search of Our Mothers' Gardens.* In the essay, which is presented in a series of flashbacks, Alice writes that she was injured while playing "Cowboys and Indians" with two of her brothers. The boys, ages ten and twelve, had BB guns that had been purchased for them by their parents. Because she was a girl, Alice, age eight, did not get a gun and was "instantly relegated to the position of Indian" with only a bow and arrow. She notes that on the day of the injury, she was on top of the family's tin-roofed carport, holding her bow and arrow, when she felt a piercing blow that blinded her right eye.

"Both brothers rush to my side. My eye stings, and I cover it with my hand," she writes. "'If you tell,' they say, 'we will get a whipping. You don't want that to happen, do you?' I do not."

The incident, as chronicled in the essay, would have a far-reaching impact on Alice's self-esteem and, ultimately, on her development as a writer. It would also lead to a painful breach fueled by the complexity of family dynamics and the vagaries of memory.

Her Brothers' Versions

It is a sunny, fall afternoon forty-three years after Alice's injury. Curtis Walker, a copper-colored man in his midfifties wearing a red running suit and white mesh loafers, sits on a chair in a disheveled convenience store in Atlanta that is both his place of business and his makeshift home. Patrons going in and out of The Lookout Chicken Fish Steak Sub Restaurant, next door, pop in and utter a low-toned "how ya' doin'" to Curtis, who has had a string of run-ins with the law and is afforded a certain sympathetic sorrow in the gritty neighborhood. But today, "Curt" is not interested in talking about his troubles with eviction notices or slick gambling buddies. Training his eyes on a can of motor oil that sits on a distant shelf, he leans forward and slowly begins another story.

"This is how it went down," said Curtis. "Mama and Daddy had got us BB guns. There was a car shelter in the yard and

Alice climbed on top of it. She had Bobby's gun. I had mine. I shot my gun and the BB rose high in the air and hit her right smack in the eye. It was a terrible accident, no doubt about it. And as far as the outcome, it doesn't make a bit of difference, but Alice had a BB gun, too. It was just one of those things that can go wrong when kids are playing."

As for Bobby, he lets loose with a torrent of words when, in a telephone conversation, he recalls that day in the yard. "I can see it as plain as if it were today," he said, his voice direct and methodic. "We were living in a house way back off the road, without hardly any neighbors, and me, Alice, and Curtis had to make up games to entertain ourselves.

"We would play with knives—throwing them and trying to get them to stick in stuff, like a sheet of writing paper. On the day Alice got shot, we were playing 'Cowboys and Indians.' I let Alice use my BB gun because Curtis was selfish. I was up on the carport with her, helping her cock the gun, and Curtis was on the ground below. Curtis pointed his gun up at us, fired, and the BB struck Alice's eye. I knew we were gonna get killed, so I told Alice to tell Mama she stepped on a wire. It was very unfortunate what happened and we all felt bad about it. It was a real sad day." . . .

Back to Normal—Except for Alice

There is no disputing the anguish that settled over the Walker household in the aftermath of the incident that left an unsightly scar and permanently damaged the vision of the sassy, outgoing child who had once happily proclaimed herself to be "the prettiest" in the family. However, contrary to their fears, neither Curtis nor Bobby ever received much punishment for their behavior. Their first line of defense was to persuade their baby sister—as pressure from the shot began to build up blinding pain inside her right eye—to tell her mother that she'd stepped on a wire that snapped back in her face. When they later confessed that Curtis had shot Alice, he and Bobby "got a mild reprimand and that was the end of the BB guns." After a while, "everything went back to normal," Curtis recalled.

But not for Alice. For her, "normal" had meant running, full-out, through the fields with her vision unhampered. It had meant smiling back at a delighted sea of black faces when, in patent leather shoes and frilly dresses, she rose before the church each spring and recited her Easter speech. "Normal" had meant being adored because she was "the icing on the cake and the ice cream, too" as her brother Bill had once lovingly described Alice.

Far from what Curtis believed, and as the entire Walker family would later come to know, for Alice the injury had devastating consequences. "It was great fun being cute," she would write in "Beauty. . ." "But then one day, it ended." . . .

Hurtful Relocation

"Now when I stare at people—a favorite pastime, up to now—they will stare back," she wrote in the essay. "Not at the 'cute' little girl, but at her scar. For six years I do not stare at anyone, because I do not raise my head."

Uprooted by her family's move from the familiar surroundings of Wards Chapel to Milledgeville, Alice also suffered the insecurity of being a newcomer at the school there, a former penitentiary with its execution chamber barely disguised. The "creepy" school deepened Alice's sense of vulnerability. And she missed the soothing purrs of her gray-and-white cat, Phoebe, astray when the Walkers left Putnam County and never found.

Alice later lamented, "All new children and teachers and that awful school with the imprint of the electric chair. I was not known. My disfigured eye was all the new children saw."

Doris Reid [a friend] remembers the dramatic shift in Alice's personality after the injury, which she says neither her parents nor the Walkers ever mentioned. "Nobody said a word about it," she maintains.

The shroud of silence was no doubt connected to the profound sense of guilt and regret Alice's parents must have felt about buying their sons BB guns and the pain (mental and physical) Alice suffered afterward. For about a month after the incident, with Alice taunted by schoolmates and her grades faltering for the first time ever, the Walkers, thinking it was best for their child, sent her back to Wards Chapel. There, she lived with her paternal grandparents and re-enrolled in East Putnam Consolidated, where she'd been the star pupil in Miss Reynolds's class. After closing shop on Fridays at Stribling's garage, Bill would routinely return Alice to Milledgeville for weekends with the family, [her sister] Ruth said.

Exiled and Isolated

"Up until the eye incident, Alice had been a straight A student, then she started bringing home Bs and Cs," Ruth explained. "The kids in Milledgeville were mean and hurtful, so Mama and Daddy wanted to protect her. With Alice back at the old school, they knew she'd be loved by Miss Reynolds, by our grandparents, and everybody else in the community. Our whole family returned to Wards Chapel that next year. So, looking at the big picture, Mama and Daddy thought they were doing more good for Alice than harm."

It *was* a relief for Alice to be spared the cruel "one-eye" invectives of her Milledgeville classmates. Still, Alice said she felt both abandoned and punished by her parents' decision to send her away from home. Why was it, she wondered, that *she* had to leave the family instead of Curtis or Bobby? To her wounded, eight-year-old spirit, the decision felt like rejection. And if not rejection, it certainly felt unfair. "My parents didn't explain why, what, when, or anything," Alice remembered. "It was decided and off I went."

Ashamed of her appearance and unable to understand why she was "exiled," her brothers left to run free, Alice became increasingly despondent and withdrawn. She took refuge in the books she received from friends and relatives at Christmas and for birthdays—*Gulliver's Travels*, *Robinson Crusoe*, and collections of fairy tales. She also began to write sad poems.

"Before, Alice was inquisitive and extremely outgoing," Reid remembered. "She was the type of child that could charm a rock. After the accident, she wanted to be more alone. She tended to be more to herself. We still had fun, but she wasn't as talkative as before and she spent a lot more time with her books. I could see those changes and because I loved Alice, they just hurt my little heart.

"I looked beyond the eye, whereas I don't think Alice did. I remember telling her, as we got older, 'Oh Alice, you look so pretty. You're just glowing,' and all this and that. And she'd say, 'Oh stop. I'm ugly. Everybody knows I'm not pretty anymore.'"

Feelings of Bitterness and Injustice

Over the years, Alice's sadness and lack of self-worth would be compounded by the sense of betrayal she felt. The way she saw it, she'd been wronged. By her brothers. By her parents. And perhaps, worst of all, by the lie her brothers had bullied her into telling to save their own hides. About their allegation that she, too, had been a "gun-wielding cowboy," half a century later, Alice would defend herself as she had not been able to do as an eight-year-old girl with a wounded eye: "My instinct is that my brothers have concocted another face-saving story. Again, it is their word against mine. If I had a gun too, the battle would seem fair. Even if I didn't know how to shoot it. At the time of the injury everyone referred to it not only as 'an accident,' but as '*my* accident'—thereby absolving my brothers of any blame.

"The unhappy truth is that I was left feeling a great deal of pain and loss and forced to think I had somehow brought it on myself. It was very like a rape. It was the first time I abandoned myself, by lying, and is at the root of my fear of abandonment. It is also the root of my need to tell the truth, always, because I experienced, very early, the pain of telling a lie."

Feeling Like an Outsider

Maria Lauret

Maria Lauret teaches American studies at the University of Sussex in Brighton, England. She is the author of Liberating Literature: Feminist Fiction in America.

Alice Walker has revealed herself in many autobiographical essays, explains Lauret in the following selection. Walker was born in Eatonton, Georgia, in 1944 to poverty-stricken farmers. She observed the sophistication of her northern aunts who came home to visit, so unlike the people she encountered in the South. Walker's childhood convinced her of a community's ability to heal individuals and also impressed upon her the need to make the oppressed her cause, asserts Lauret. Yet, as a writer, Walker knew that life for an African American woman in the South should never be romanticized. Although Walker had a close relationship with her mother, she felt bullied and devalued by the men in her family. Lauret concludes that even after being educated at Spelman College and Sarah Lawrence and moving from the South, Walker felt that she was an outsider—not only among women writers but also among African American writers.

The Color Purple dresses its shocking contents in something like the 'folkspants' that Celie sews: custom made, yet 'one size fits all'. Perhaps it is because of this ironic contrast between Celie's innocent voice and what that voice tells us that critics have found so much to say about *The Color Purple* and yet have contradicted each other so frequently. One size does, indeed, fit all, but the question is what *specifically* individual readers see in a novel of abuse, rape, incest, battery and exploitation. What is the pleasure of this text? How is it that *The*

Maria Lauret, "Chapter Four: *The Color Purple*," in *Modern Novelists: Alice Walker*. New York: St. Martin's Press, 2000, pp. 91–95, 97, 110–13. Copyright © 2000 St. Martin's Press. All rights reserved. Reproduced by permission.

Color Purple has become—with *Beloved* [the 1987 Pulitzer Prize–winning novel by Toni Morrison]—*the* teaching novel of choice in the (still emerging) canon of African American women's writing? . . .

Scores of articles have been written about [*The Color Purple*], every critical anthology of feminist literary scholarship contains multiple references to it, and the release of [producer and director] Steven Spielberg's film yielded a whole new crop of journalistic and academic responses, as well as protest marches and public debates. *The Color Purple* seemed a most unlikely text to be adopted by the mainstream, given the controversial nature of its political and sexual content. . . .

Contradictions and Questions

This story [of the novel], even, when told as neutrally as I can tell it, is full of holes, unlikelihoods and strange coincidences and any literal-minded reader would be left with lots of questions. Why did Celie's letters return unopened? How can an abused woman reconcile herself with the husband who treated her like dirt, and come to love his mistress? Why has no one else ever told Celie about her real parents? How likely is it, really, that a black woman is allowed a successful business venture (making unisex trousers, of all things) if we are also asked to accept that her father was lynched for just such an enterprise? And isn't it a little too convenient that an inheritance should arrive just as Celie needs it to make her happiness complete? All these are questions which arise in the mind of anyone who is looking for more than merely a sob-story which turns out well in the end, a reader who wants a mode of telling it which will make it coherent, or someone who is looking for role models in this feminist fable. After all, the epigraph to the novel is [blind musical artist] Stevie Wonder's 'show me how to do like you/show me how to do it', and seems to invite such an inspirational reading. None of those wishes is on first reading fulfilled. There is a lot of vagueness too, about time and place and the historical details of the relation between Africa and America. Why does Nettie go to 'Africa', rather than to a specific country or region of that vast continent? Did the Olinka really exist? Why is the novel not apparently set in a real time frame (for example, the first forty-five years or so of the twentieth century) and in a real place, but are both collapsed into some fantasy space and history? . . .

Most critics regard *The Color Purple* as an historical novel of some sort, because it is set in a time which clearly is not the present, but which is only in a generalised way 'the' past. This past we cannot pin down very accurately except by using historical markers such as the appearance of automobiles and mention of a global war. Because *The Color Purple* does not seem to care too much about historical facticity, [author] Lauren Berlant argues that it offers a critical rewrite of the historical novel. As such it is not concerned with the public history of war and conquest, but with domestic strife and victory: a women's version of the historical novel, in other words. [African American writer] Darryl Pinckney situates its setting the inter-war period, but adds that '[T]he novel, . . . with its flat characters, sudden revelations, and moral tags, has a doggedly nineteenth century quality.' . . .

The African American Feminist Context

Critics note, *The Color Purple* completes a feminist project which [Harlem Renaissance writer] Zora Neale Hurston had begun. And wherever orality and literacy are highlighted, silence figures too—as a trope which traditionally has been associated with the sexually abused woman. This adds a further layer of signification to Celie's troubled discourse and allies her with Marguerite in [author] Maya Angelou's *I Know Why the Caged Bird Sings*, who is silent for several years after she has been raped by her stepfather: women writers write what abused girls cannot speak. [Literary scholar] Christine Froula,

In her writing, Alice Walker often credits great women blues singers like Mamie Smith (pictured). Getty Images.

in a psychoanalytic reading, sees Celie's letters as a breaking of the patriarchal taboo on women speaking out about abuse. . . .

The conjunction of Alice Walker and the blues is, of course, no coincidence. Walker has often credited the great women blues singers (Ma Rainey, Bessie Smith, Mamie Smith) in her work, and the short-story collection *You Can't Keep a*

Good Woman Down is dedicated to them 'for insisting on the value and beauty of the authentic' as well as deriving its title from a Mamie Smith song ('You Can't Keep a Good Man Down'). The short story 'Nineteen Fifty-Five' takes as its subject the misappropriation of a black woman's blues song by a white male singer, Traynor, who looks remarkably like Elvis Presley. . . .

In *The Color Purple* . . . the cultural significance of Shug's occupation goes beyond its mere narrative importance, because Shug evokes a whole tradition of women's cultural activity and self-assertion. As a blues singer Shug can teach Celie a lesson in sexual autonomy and desire, which is part of Walker's womanist philosophy for which Shug is the mouthpiece throughout. She also wields the power of economic independence over Albert, which means that he cannot control her as he can Celie. Conversely, though, and much more obliquely, Celie, the archetypal victim, also educates Shug in the ethics, if not the aesthetics, of everyday use. For everyday use is what Celie is to Mr _____, and also to Shug when they first meet: a doormat, nurse, nanny and cook combined. Shug has to learn to *see* Celie first, and then to value her dignity and integrity over and above her labour—a 'weepy miracle' indeed.

Walker's Influences

It has been suggested (by Henry Louis Gates, and also by Walker herself in an interview) that feisty, sassy and outrageous Zora Neale Hurston herself was the model for Shug, but there are plenty of other likely originals available in the long line of hard-living, hard-loving women blues singers such as Ma Rainey, Ethel Waters, Bessie Smith, Mamie Smith, Trixie Smith and others, not called Smith. In the autobiography of a good friend of Zora Neale Hurston, Ethel Waters's *His Eye Is on the Sparrow*, we find numerous examples of the kind of blues discourse which inspires Celie's. When Waters writes:

'We are close to this earth and to God.[...] Our greatest elo-
quence ... comes when we lift up our faces and talk to God,
person to person', it is almost as if she gives a description of
The Color Purple, for talking to God 'person to person' is what
Celie does in her early letters. And lines such as 'Any God you
worship is good if he brings you love.[...] His is almost like
an inner voice, soothing and calming' sound like they could
have been spoken by Shug. Talking to God does not usually
characterise the blues, which is regarded as a secular musical
form, unlike the gospel songs discussed in the previous chapter. And indeed, Celie's discourse is secularised as her relationship with Shug develops and she is able to *tell* rather than
write. Her development echoes that of Janie in Hurston's
Their Eyes Were Watching God, who tells her friend Pheoby at
the end about the 'Two things everybody's got tuh do fuh
theyselves. They got tuh go tuh God, and they got tuh find
out about livin' fuh theyselves.' In Waters's autobiography we
hear the voices of Shug, Celie and Zora mingled, singing in
close harmony. Waters asks: 'if anyone could be so banged
around and unloved during childhood days and still come out
of it whole, a complete person'. This is a blues question, answered in *The Color Purple* with a resounding 'yes'.

'Banged around and unloved during childhood days' is not
just Celie's and Ethel Waters's story, but that of many of
Walker's characters (Brownfield Copeland, Meridian, Daughter
in 'The Child Who Favored Daughter') and, indeed, of Walker
herself. Blues musicians' autobiographies, and African American autobiographies which use the blues discourse as a ver-
nacular articulation of suffering, often begin with such an account of childhood trauma and neglect. The opening lines of
His Eye Is on the Sparrow could come out of a Walker novel,
essay, or short story:

I never was a child.

I never was coddled, or liked, or understood
by my family.

I never felt I belonged.

I was always an outsider.

I was born out of wedlock, but that had nothing to do with all this.

To people like mine a thing like that just didn't mean much.

Nobody brought me up. (my emphasis)

The Color Purple and Women's Issues

From Being Dominated to Taking Charge

Donna Haisty Winchell

Donna Haisty Winchell of Clemson University is the coauthor of Elements of Argument *(2005).*

According to Winchell in this essay, at the start of Celie's narrative, when she is virtually a slave, she is able to endure the physical and psychological abuse of her father, and then of her husband, by talking to "Old Maker," a God who is white and male. Despite the sick divide between men and women and the oppression of Celie by Albert, Alice Walker has indicated that she intended for Albert to be more sympathetic at the end than audiences regard him. Winchell asserts that Celie's and Albert's mutual love for Shug, ironically, brings them a little closer together for a time. But with the discovery that Albert has hidden her sister's letters from her, Shug helps Celie leave Albert and begin to replace the traditional God with a genderless God of the earth. In Winchell's view, the universality of women's subjugation is emphasized by the descriptions of abuse of women in Africa, but eventually gender distinctions begin to be modified in Celie's community and healing begins.

In a scene reminiscent of a slave auction, Celie's stepfather . . . offers her in marriage to the widower Albert ———, who looks her over like a head of livestock and marries her in desperation because he needs someone to cook and clean for him and take care of his four children. Thus Celie is passed like a piece of property from one cruel and domineering black male into the hands of another. The rest of the novel is Celie's struggle to gain self-respect. At first fighting back does not

Donna Haisty Winchell, "Chapter Seven: Letters to God: *The Color Purple*," in *Alice Walker*. New York: Twayne Publishers, 1992, pp. 86–99. Copyright © 1992 Gale, a part of Cengage Learning Inc. Reproduced by permission.

even seem an option; survival seems the best she can hope for, in this world at least. She stands silent, like a tree, as Mr. —— beats her, thinking, "That's how come I know trees fear man." Death seems the only way out of a miserable existence, as Celie tells her daughter-in-law Sofia: "Well, sometime Mr. —— git on me pretty hard. I have to talk to Old Maker. But he my husband. I shrug my shoulders. This life soon be over, I say. Heaven last always." Sofia's response provides Celie with a rare moment of humor: "You ought to bash Mr. —— head open, she say. Think bout heaven later." Celie thinks, "Not much funny to me. That funny."

Finding Her God

Celie's ability eventually to stand up to and leave Mr. —— —— is due in part to her discovering a definition of God that is large enough to encompass even the poor, ugly black woman that she feels herself to be and in part to her discovering within herself the ability to love and be loved.

Love is noticeably absent from much of Celie's early life. The one person who loves Celie, her younger sister, Nettie, is torn from her when Nettie is first forced from her home by her stepfather's sexual advances and then from Celie's home when she rejects Mr. ——'s. . . .

Diseased Sex Roles

Walker argues . . . that what her critics have failed to see is that Mister, too, changes, that the novel is about the dis-ease that both Celie and Albert —— suffer from, an illness that derives from the experiences that early shaped their personalities and from their culturally derived sex roles. Walker writes, "They proceed to grow, to change, to become whole, i.e., well, by becoming more like each other, but stopping short of taking on each other's illness." In a 1985 interview in *Ms.*, Walker acknowledges that a feminist director might have made different choices in presenting Celie and her husband, "but Steven

[Spielberg], I think, was more interested in showing the transformation of Mister to Albert, as well as Celie's changes ... I think you really understand Albert better in the movie than in the book." She admits in "In the Closet of the Soul" that she indeed loves Albert because he "went deeply enough into himself to find the courage to change. To grow." Celie too goes inside herself to find the courage to change and grow.

Coming to Know the God Within

Primary among the experiences that shape Celie's personality is her mistreatment by men. Out of these experiences grows her disdain for men and, later, for the traditional God modeled in their image.

Early it becomes obvious that she feels little for men except fear. When her stepfather beats her for allegedly winking at a boy in church, she writes, "I don't even look at mens. That's the truth. I look at women, tho, cause I'm not scared of them." When, after her marriage, another black woman compliments Albert's good looks, Celie writes, "He do look all right, I say. But I don't think about it while I say it. Most times mens look pretty much alike to me." Sex with Albert holds no pleasure for her, as she tells Shug Avery, Albert's long-time lover. . . .

Celie's feelings toward men do not initially prevent her accepting without question a God created in the image of man, albeit a white man. At Shug's insistence, she describes what her God looks like: a "big and old and tall and graybearded" white man in long white robes. When Shug laughs, Celie asks, "Why you laugh? . . . What you expect him to look like, Mr. ———?" Celie is not able to redefine herself in any but a subservient position until she replaces her fear of men with anger and, in the process, redefines God. . . .

Celie is not in a literal sense a slave, but she certainly is "sexually abused, . . . whipped, the mother of children she could not want, lover of children she could not have." In her suffering, as hundreds of slave women before her she finds the twin self within. The letters that constitute the first half of the novel are a one-way correspondence between the abused and lonely Celie and her own inner self—that part of herself that eventually makes her fight back. In writing to God she is writing to the part of her personality growing progressively stronger until she is able to acknowledge the God within herself and demand the respect due her.

First, though, she has to reject her traditional notions of divinity. This she does with the help of Shug Avery. . . .

Love Between Women

Where Celie is not at all attracted to men, she is immediately drawn to Shug, who has been her husband's lover for years. Shug and Albert never married because his lightskinned father disapproved of Shug's dark skin; now her own father considers her a tramp because she has had three children by a man she never married and makes her living singing in juke joints. Celie begins to dream of Shug, though, from the moment she first sees a picture of her. Rather than being pushed farther apart when Albert brings Shug into their home to recuperate from what the town gossips suspect is "some nasty woman disease," Celie and Albert find that their mutual love for Shug draws them closer than ever before.

Celie finds herself aroused by Shug in a way that no man has ever aroused her. Her sexual attraction to Shug is clear the first time she bathes the ailing Shug and feels that she has turned into a man as she gazes at Shug's naked body, feeling that washing her body is a sort of prayer. Looking at Shug's thin black hands, she can hardly resist the temptation to take Shug's fingers into her mouth. She still feels no sexual stirrings for Albert even when they "make love," but the mere thought of Shug is enough to make her feel "something stirring down there." The only reason she even tries to find some meager joy in sex with Mister is that she knows it is something Shug has shared with him—and liked.

Once Shug succeeds in awakening Celie to her own sexuality, Celie only agonizes more to realize that while she loves Shug, Shug loves Albert. She tries to convince herself that "that the way it spose to be," but her heart hurts just the same, and she cries as she overhears Shug and Albert making love. Soon, however, she is crying in Shug's arms instead, and talking about love. . . .

Finding a Genderless, Personal God

Celie rejects her own former notion of a white and male God in anger when she learns, with Shug's assistance, that Albert has "stolen" Nettie from her by hiding her letters. Finally reading through the stacks of old letters, Celie learns her real father was lynched and the man she knew as her father was really her stepfather. She is understandably relieved to learn that her children are not her own brother and sister, yet she is angered by all that God has allowed to happen to her. She no longer writes to God and even denies his existence as she explains to Shug why she doesn't.

What God do for me? I ast.

She say, Celie! Like she shock. He give you life, good health, and a good woman that love you to death.

Yeah, I say, and he give me a lynched daddy, a crazy mama, a lowdown dog of a step pa and a sister I probably won't ever see again. Anyhow, I say, the God I been praying and writing to is a man. And act just like all the other mens I know. Trifling, forgitful and lowdown.

She say, Miss Celie, You better hush. God might hear you.

Let 'im hear me, I say. If he ever listened to poor colored women the world would be a different place, I can tell you.

Celie is ready now to accept the genderless God that Shug offers her. Shug points out that she too lost interest in God when she discovered that He was white, and a man. She continues,

> Here's the thing, says Shug. The thing I believe. God is inside you and inside everybody else. You come into the world with God. But only them that search for it inside find it. . . .
>
> It? I ast.
>
> Yeah, It. God ain't a he or a she, but a It.
>
> But what do it look like? I ast.
>
> Don't look like nothing, she say. It ain't a picture show. It ain't something you can look at apart from anything else, including yourself. I believe God is everything, say Shug. Everything that is or ever was or ever will be. And when you can feel that, and be happy to feel that, you've found It. . . .

She will enter creation by becoming one with all created things, and in her climactic and mystical departure scene she does. She takes on seemingly God-like powers when she curses Mister before going to Memphis with Shug. As she confronts her husband, warning him that all the suffering that he has inflicted on her will be inflicted on him twofold, it is not her voice she hears, but the trees and the wind and the dirt speaking through her. In still another sense, she will enter creation by becoming a creator herself. Tempted at one point to slit Mister's throat for all the evil that he has done, she chooses the needle over the razor and takes advantage of her skill as a seamstress to enter the world of business. As God does when his efforts are taken for granted, she sets out to create something new. . . .

Parallels Between African and Southern Black Women

Nettie serves as a convenient audience to replace the God that Celie has rejected (with the exception of the last letter, which, in its salutation, reflects Celie's newfound pantheism: "Dear God. Dear stars, dear trees, dear sky, dear peoples. Dear Everyting. Dear God." The remainder of the novel consists of Nettie's accumulated letters and the letters to Nettie that now replace Celie's letters to God. Nettie's letters, in their formal English, seem stiffly didactic after the poetic beauty of Celie's nearly illiterate attempts to verbalize her plight, but they provide a parallel between the oppressive, male-dominated Southern society that Celie has now become strong enough to rebel against and an equally oppressive and male-dominated society in Africa.

Celie's daughter, Olivia, is allowed to go to school in Africa, but education is denied the native Olinka girls. Women are expected to fulfill a subservient role in their village, never looking directly into a man's face. They are defined only in terms of the value they have for their husbands. Nettie is told by one of the Olinka women, "A girl is nothing to herself; only to her husband can she become something." Nettie asks, "What can she become?" and is told, "The mother of his children." Nettie compares the power the Olinka man has over his wife to the power their stepfather had over her and Celie, and the general desire of the African society to keep women uneducated to the desire of American whites to keep blacks ignorant. The final horror for Nettie and her niece and nephew is the clitoridectomy required of young African women as part of their initiation into adulthood.

According to feminist Mary Daly, some African cultures perform the clitoridectomy in an attempt to remove that which is masculine from the female genitalia. Wall adds that such genital mutilation is thus an attempt to suggest that gender differentiation is socially inscribed. She continues, "Throughout *The Color Purple*, inherent biological gender characteristics are questioned; gender becomes a socially-imposed categorization." This interpretation is in keeping with Walker's claim that both Celie and Albert exist in a state of dis-ease because of socially defined sex roles. They become whole and at peace only when they achieve an androgynous blend of traditionally male and female characteristics. Gender sharing and gender crossover eventually allow Celie and Albert to grow toward wholeness by growing more like each other.

Reversal of Sex Roles

Reversal of gender roles is initially most obvious in the characters Harpo, Albert's son, and Sofia, Harpo's wife. Even as Harpo grows into manhood, Celie, his stepmother, notices that his face begins to look like a woman's face. As soon as Harpo marries the big, strong, and ruddy-looking Sofia, who has already borne him a child, Mister predicts that she will soon switch the traces on him, and she does. Sofia is at home in a man's pants, splitting shingles and working on the roof. (This scene recalls images from Nettie's letter reporting that in the Olinka village the job of thatching roofs belongs to the women.) She prefers field work and even chopping wood to keeping house. (In Africa, Nettie informs Celie, the women are responsible for the crops.) The irony is that Harpo truly enjoys "woman's work," and the two could have been quite content with him cooking and washing dishes and her doing traditional men's work had Mister not raised Harpo to feel less of a man if he was not in control. Harpo cannot simply accept that he and Sofia are happy in their reversed roles—and that love is a far more important element in marriage than obedience—but must rather try to prove his manhood by beating her, as Mister beats Celie, to make her "mind." They fight "like two mens," with Harpo constantly getting the worst of the beating. When he gorges himself with food in an attempt to grow as big as Sofia, he only looks pregnant. "When it due? us ast."

Sofia finally loses interest in Harpo and, with their five children in tow, leaves him. She eventually goes to jail for striking the white mayor, surviving there only by masking her own natural aggression and pretending instead to be the meek and submissive Miss Celie. When at the end of the novel Harpo and Sofia are together again, they revert to the roles that they are most comfortable with even if society is not, with Sofia clerking in the store that Celie has inherited from her real father and Harpo staying at home.

Celie and Shug, of course, cross traditional gender boundaries as soon as they enter into their lesbian relationship. There is something of the masculine in Shug, in spite of all her flamboyant, feminine charm. She is, for one thing, totally inept at sewing. Shug's mother is raising Shug's three children. Even Celie acknowledges that Shug is manly in her talk at times. . . .

Easing of Gender Antagonism

To get Celie's mind off of killing Mister once she learns that he has been hiding Nettie's letters, Shug encourages her to make some pants. In fact, she encourages her to wear pants because, as she tells Celie, "You don't have a dress do nothing for you. You not made like no dress pattern either." Celie assumes that Mister will not permit his wife to wear pants, but she learns, to her surprise, that Shug used to put on Albert's pants when they were courting—that they were "like a red flag to a bull"—and that, once, he even put on her dress. When Celie leaves Albert to move to Memphis with Shug, she soon finds that she can make a living by practicing the traditionally feminine art of sewing, but the pants that she quickly becomes famous for are equally appropriate for men and women. Back home, Mister sinks into such a state of self-pity and drunkenness that Harpo takes over the traditionally feminine duties of cooking and cleaning for him, and even bathing him. At one point Sofia walks in to find Harpo and his father asleep in each other's arms.

Walker has been accused of painting men in a favorable light only when they become too old to be a threat sexually. Celie's heart softens toward Harpo when she hears how he cared for Mister. The extent to which men become likeable is directly proportional, then, not to their age, but rather to the extent to which they take on feminine characteristics. The change in the heart of Albert is almost as hard to believe in as the change in the heart of Grange Copeland [in another of Walker's novels], but as Celie eventually has to admit, "If you know your heart [is] sorry . . . that mean it not quite as spoilt as you think." At the end of the novel Albert is working his fields once again and keeping house for himself, even cooking. He appears late in the novel sewing with Celie on the porch of the house they once shared and actually designing shirts to go with Celie's pants. He recalls that as a child he liked to sew along with his mother until others ridiculed him. Celie tells him that in Africa, after all, men quilt and wear "dresses." She is the one now wearing the pants and smoking a pipe.

Race in Black Women's Issues

[Literary scholar] Bernard Bell has pointed out that *The Color Purple* is "more concerned with the politics of sex and self than with the politics of class and race. . . . its unrelenting, severe attacks on male hegemony, especially the violent abuse of black women by black men, is offered as a revolutionary leap forward into a new social order based on sexual egalitarianism." A part of the self Albert must contend with, however, is undeniably racial, and a part of his acceptance of self is an ability to love that part of himself that his own partially white father most hates.

One of Walker's disappointments with the response to her works has been that many black men proved themselves incapable of empathizing with the black woman's suffering under sexism, but also that, even worse, with *The Color Purple* they seized the opportunity presented by the publicity surrounding the book and the movie to draw attention to themselves as though they were the ones being oppressed. Related to the denial that such sexual brutality exists in the black community is the refusal to accept the fact that blacks are in many cases descended not only from slaves, but also from slave owners. . . .

The Healing

Celie has never before been at such peace with Albert or with herself. They have shared the sorrow of having lost Shug to someone else. Now Celie knows that she can bear life with or without Shug: "If she come, I be happy. If she don't, I be content. And then I figure this the lesson I was suppose to learn." Celie is also at peace with God, a point she makes as she explains to an understandably stunned Sofia why she smokes marijuana. "I smoke when I want to talk to God. I smoke when I want to make love. Lately I feel like me and God make love just fine anyhow. Whether I smoke reefer or not."

"Miss Celie! say Sofia. Shock. Girl, I'm bless, I say to Sofia. God knows what I mean."

Ntozake Shange's closing words in [her play] *for colored girls who have considered suicide when the rainbow is enuf* would be fitting ones for Celie at this advanced stage of her psychological development: "i found god in myself and i loved her fiercely."

Being Deprived of a Mother's Bond

Charles L. Proudfit

Charles L. Proudfit is professor emeritus of English at the University of Colorado at Boulder and the author of articles on Alice Walker and Stephen Crane.

In the following article, Proudfit provides a reading of The Color Purple *using the findings of psychologist D.W. Winnicott, whose thesis is that the relationship between mother and child in infancy has repercussions for the rest of the child's life. According to this view, even a "good-enough" mother is better than no mother at all or a completely ineffectual one. The rupture in Celie's childhood relationship with her mother fills her with loneliness, shame, depression, and deep-seated rage. As a result, Proudfit argues, the adult Celie has no sense of self. Nor does Celie's younger sister, Nettie, have any sense of her true self, having lacked a mother, a sister, and her own culture. Celie finally finds her voice and her identity through bonding with surrogate mothers, primarily Shug. Proudfit argues that the ending, in which both sisters find closure by reuniting with each other and the substitute mothers, is psychologically valid.*

Since the publication of Alice Walker's *The Color Purple*, both novel and author continue to elicit a wide range of praise and censure from an increasing number of black and white, female and male reviewers, literary critics, and general readers. At one extreme are those who find the work "an American novel of permanent importance," who place the author "in the company of [William] Faulkner"; and who praise

Charles L. Proudfit, "Celie's Search for Identity: A Psychoanalytic Developmental Reading of Alice Walker's *The Color Purple*," *Contemporary Literature*, vol. 32, no. 1, 1991, pp. 12–14, 17–19, 22–24, 31–33. Copyright © 1991 by The University of Wisconsin Press. Reproduced by permission.

Walker for her creation of the unique voice of her protagonist, Celie, a "poor, ugly, uneducated [black girl] . . . [from] rural Georgia," for "the universality of the themes of redemptive love, strength in adversity, independence, and self-assertion through the values of community," and for "creating a unique set of people who speak to the *human* condition." At the other extreme are those who feel that the novel should be "ignored" rather than "canonized"; who place Walker "closer to Harriet Beecher Stowe than to [Zora Neale] Hurston"; and who censure Walker for the creation of an unrealistic plot, for the "depiction of violent black men who physically and psychologically abuse their wives and children . . . [and for the] depiction of lesbianism," and for peopling her novel with characters who "themselves do not seem to respond to [some form of] internal logic." Walker herself relates that her mother finds the book's language "offensive" and humorously describes a parent's attempt to have the novel banned in a California public school system. Between these extreme critical positions, one finds a growing body of measured literary criticism that addresses both the novel's formal qualities and thematic concerns and that validates the novel's having been awarded in 1983 both the American Book Award for Fiction and the Pulitzer Prize. . . .

The Importance of the Mother-Daughter Bond

This reading is based upon a mother-daughter bond that, according to several current psychoanalytic theorists on female development, has its origins in deep, primitive ties to the mother of infancy and is a bond that must be worked through *again and again during a woman's lifetime*. Walker's descriptions of Celie's bonding, first with the biological mother of infancy and later with suitable mother surrogates, is psychologically realistic and ranges from the ministrations of Celie's younger sister Nettie, to Kate and Sofia, and to Shug's facilitat-

In this scene from the film adaptation of Alice Walker's novel The Color Purple, *Celie Johnson (Whoopi Goldberg, left) bonds with Shug Avery (Margaret Avery, right), who acts as a surrogate mother for Celie.* © The Picture Desk.

ing Celie's sensual awakening to adult female sexuality and a healthy emotional life. This "female bonding," which occurs over an extended period of time, enables Celie—a depressed survivor-victim of parent loss, emotional and physical neglect, rape, incest, trauma, and spousal abuse—to resume her arrested development and continue developmental processes that were thwarted in infancy and early adolescence. These processes are described with clinical accuracy; and, as they are revisited and reworked in Celie's interactions with appropriate mother surrogates, Celie is enabled to get in touch with her feelings, work through old traumas, and achieve an emotional maturity and a firm sense of identity that is psychologically convincing. . . .

Shame and Rage of the Victim

Walker, like [nineteenth-century novelist] Charlotte Brontë in *Jane Eyre* (one of Walker's favorite novels in childhood) begins *The Color Purple in medias res* [in the middle of things]: Celie, like Jane, is poised on the edge of adolescence after a childhood of loss, deprivation, and abuse. With Celie's first anguished letter to God, Walker enables the reader to enter into the private thoughts and emotional state of her traumatized, guilt- and shame-ridden, and depressed fourteen-year-old protagonist, who has been repeatedly raped and impregnated by the man (Alphonso) whom she believes to be her biological father: "Dear God, I am fourteen years old. I have always been a good girl. Maybe you can give me a sign letting me know what is happening to me." Celie draws a line through "I am" and writes "I have always been a good girl," because the child victim of rape and incest often blames herself for her trauma; or, worse still, believes that this bad thing has happened to her because *she* is bad and therefore deserves it. Celie writes to God because she is ashamed of what is happening to her and because of the threat from Alphonso that immediately precedes Celie's first letter: "*You better not never tell nobody but God. It'd kill your mammy.*" Threats and forced secrecy are usual parts of incest. . . .

Celie as a Motherless Child

In Celie's second letter, written about a year later, Celie's mother has died, screaming and cursing her pregnant daughter. After the birth of Celie's second child, Alphonso gives her infant son away, as he had her infant daughter, though Celie believes that he has killed them. She stops menstruating after the second birth. During the next five years, Celie lives at home with Alphonso, his new young wife, and a growing number of their children; she serves as a maid, and as protector of her younger sister Nettie against Alphonso's sexual advances. At twenty, Celie is married off to Albert, a widower with children, who also abuses her. Nettie joins them but is soon told by Albert to leave.

It is not until sometime later, when Albert brings home his old flame Shug Avery, that Celie is enabled, with Shug's help, to find Nettie's letters to her. These letters, written after Nettie goes to live with the missionaries Corrine and Samuel but hidden by Albert, reveal to Celie the truth of her origin. She discovers that Alphonso is not her biological father and that she lived for the first two years of her life as the only child in a loving family. The father adored his pregnant wife and, we would expect, his daughter Celie. But one night, when she was barely two years old, her successful father's store and blacksmith shop were burned and destroyed; he and his two brothers were dragged from their homes and hanged by jealous white merchants; and, when his mutilated and burned body was brought home to his wife by neighbors, she gave birth to Nettie and suffered an emotional breakdown. . . .

In a single evening, the two-year-old Celie experiences several catastrophic losses: (1) the death of a loving father; (2) the emotional loss of a loving mother (at first through a psychotic episode and later through sickness and depression); (3) the loss of a safe and nurturing family environment; and (4) the loss of her place as an only child. During the next several months, Celie and her newborn baby sister Nettie experience hunger, neglect, and other deprivations. When Alphonso appears on the scene within the year and "lavished all his attention on the widow and her children," Celie's and Nettie's physical needs were probably met, but their mentally unstable, ill, and often pregnant mother would not have been able to provide either of her daughters with the "good-enough mothering" that they needed. Given the description of Alphonso in Celie's early letters, he would not have been temperamentally fit to serve as a mother substitute. We can reasonably postulate that Celie became mother surrogate to Nettie, as well as to her ill and half-crazed mother's unwanted babies. When Celie's mother goes "to visit her sister doctor over Macon," Alphonso rapes Celie and begins to use her as a sexual replacement for his exhausted wife—a not uncommon situation in actual cases of father-daughter incest. . . .

Desperate Need for a Mother

Perhaps most important for Celie's ability to bond successfully with females in adolescence and young adulthood, and thus to resume her development of an identity, of a "True Self," is her partial but incomplete resolution of a transitional developmental phase that occurs roughly between six and twenty-four months. . . . If the mother is understanding and empathetic at this difficult time, the infant will, in the third year, go on to develop a stable sense of self and others. If, however, there are serious maternal failures . . . the developmental tasks of adolescence, especially the finalizing of gender identity and a firm sense of self, will be made even more difficult. Since Celie loses her "good-enough mother" at the height of her "rapprochement crisis," when she has yet to develop stable conscious and unconscious images of mother and her identity formation is in the early stages of development, it is hardly surprising that Celie should later respond to the ministrations of women and resume the developmental tasks of separation, autonomy, and identity formation.

Although the white, patriarchal God Celie writes to in the first part of the novel never sends her a sign, life does—primarily in the form of caring and nurturing black women. These "good-enough mothers," with the notable exception of Shug Avery, take the initiative; they intuit the depressed and traumatized Celie's deeply buried needs and break through her defensive passivity. When Nettie runs away from home to escape Alphonso's unwanted sexual advances and joins Celie and Albert, she teaches Celie "spelling and everything else she think I need to know . . . to teach me what go on in the world."

Nettie not only tries to give Celie the tools that will free her, she also, even more importantly, conveys to Celie her belief that Celie is of value. Kate, one of Albert's sisters, convinces him of Celie's need for clothes and takes her to a store to select cloth so that a dress can be made. When Celie is overcome with emotion and cannot speak, Kate reassures her and says: "You deserve more than this. Maybe so, I think." And when Sofia, Harpo's wife and Albert's daughter-in-law, suggests that Celie and she make quilt pieces, Celie writes: "I run git my pattern book. I sleeps like a baby now."

It is the seemingly inappropriate nightclub singer Shug Avery, however, who provides Celie with an extended period of "female bonding"; who, with unconditional love, provides a "holding environment" in which Celie's nascent self is reflected back to itself; and, who, as surrogate and "good-enough mother," and lover, helps Celie to complete the development of those capacities that enable her to deal more effectively with loss, to finalize her gender identity and choice of mature love object, and to develop a stable sense of self. One might argue that the development of a nurturing and positive relationship between these two women is improbable. Celie, until she hears Shug's name spoken, appears as a passive victim. After she is married to Albert, women who become mother surrogates have to reach out to her. How then can Shug's name and her picture, provided to her by Alphonso's new wife, mobilize the depressed and passive Celie actively to seek a "good-enough mother" in Shug? And when the two women meet for the first time, the deathly ill Shug's first words are "You sure *is* ugly". . . .

Nettie's Loss of a Mother

When Nettie's infancy is compared with Celie's, it is obvious that each is born into a "different family" and that each has a strikingly different developmental history. Whereas Celie spends the first two years of her life in an intact, loving, traditional family with "good-enough mothering," Nettie spends the first several months of her life experiencing severe physical and emotional deprivation and the first several years complying with the emotional needs of a depressed and mentally unstable mother. Although Celie was in all probability able to offer some mothering to Nettie in the early as well as the later

years, she could not have been a "good-enough mother" ...
Thus it is reasonable to speculate that Nettie, in order to survive, quickly learned to comply with her environment; out of necessity she developed a "False Self" at the expense of her "True Self." The text appears to corroborate this speculation.

During Nettie's adolescent years, first at home with Alphonso and later with Celie and Albert, Celie encourages Nettie "to keep at her books" in order to escape her older sister's fate—and Nettie complies. When Albert decides that Nettie has to leave, Celie tells her to look up the wife of the "Reverend Mr. _____"—and Nettie complies. And when Samuel and Corrine ask Nettie if she would like to join them in their African missionary enterprise, Nettie accepts, "But only if they would teach me everything they knew to make me useful as a missionary ... and my real education began at that time". . . .

In the next-to-last scene of *The Color Purple*, Celie's "True Self" and Nettie's "False Self," as well as their family and loved ones, are reunited. Although [literary scholar] Trudier Harris calls this a "fairy-tale" ending, I believe that the reunification scene offers a psychological validity that transcends the contrivance of plot, and that this psychological validity consists in offering closure to the developmental processes that began with the sisters' births.

The Myth of the Rape and Silencing of Philomela Informs *The Color Purple*

Martha J. Cutter

Martha J. Cutter is a professor in the English Department and the Institute for African American Studies at the University of Connecticut. She is the author of Unruly Tongue: Language and Identity in American Women's Writing *and the editor of the journal* MELUS: Multi-Ethnic Literature in the United States.

In this essay Cutter uses the myth of Philomela to expand on women's issues in The Color Purple. *In Greek mythology Philomela was raped by her brother-in-law, who subsequently cut out her tongue to silence her. Rape becomes the ultimate literal and symbolic act of violent male domination, claims Cutter. Its heinousness, recognized by aggressors and victims, leads rapists to silence their victims, as when Celie's stepfather orders her not to tell anyone what he is doing to her. The symbols of blood and birds also connect Celie with Philomela. Philomela's sister kills her son and feeds him to her husband as revenge, and both sisters are turned into birds. Celie is, herself, identified with birds throughout the text by Shug and Mister, and blood resonates throughout her story, finally turning into a positive symbol of creativity as red and purple are incorporated into most of her sewing.*

The ancient story of Philomela has resonated in the imaginations of women writers for several thousand years. The presence of this myth in contemporary texts by African American women writers marks the persistence of a powerful arche-

Martha J. Cutter, "Philomela Speaks: Alice Walker's Revisioning of Rape Archetypes in *The Color Purple*," *MELUS: Society for the Study of the Multi-Ethnic Literature of the United States*, vol. 25, Fall–Winter 2000. Copyright © 2000 by MELUS: Society for the Study of the Multi-Ethnic Literature of the United States. Reproduced by permission.

typal narrative explicitly connecting rape (a violent inscription of the female body), silencing, and the complete erasure of feminine subjectivity. For in most versions of this myth Philomela is not only raped—she is also silenced. In [Roman poet] Ovid's recounting, for example, Philomela is raped by her brother-in-law, Tereus, who then tears out her tongue. Philomela is finally transformed into a nightingale, doomed to chirp out the name of her rapist for eternity: *tereu, tereu.* The mythic narrative of Philomela therefore explicitly intertwines rape, silencing, and the destruction of feminine subjectivity.

The Doom of the Raped African American Woman in Literature

Contemporary African American women's fiction contains allusions to this archetypal rape narrative. In Toni Morrison's *The Bluest Eye,* for example, Pecola Breedlove's rape by her father Cholly causes a fragmentation of her psyche. Pecola's attempts to tell of her rape are nullified by her disbelieving mother, and by the novel's conclusion her voice is only exercised in internal colloquies with an imaginary friend. She flutters along the edges of society, a "winged but grounded bird." Similarly, in Gloria Naylor's *The Women of Brewster Place,* after Lorraine is gagged and brutally gang raped, she becomes both insane and unable to speak of her rape. Finally, she is left with only one word, a word that echoes back to Philomela's "*tereu, tereu,*" the word she attempted to use to stop her attackers: "Please. Please." Rape is thus a central trope in these texts for the mechanisms whereby a patriarchal society writes oppressive dictates on women's bodies and minds, destroying both subjectivity and voice. Or, as [literary critic] Madonne Miner puts it, "Men, potential rapists, assume presence, language, and reason as their particular province. Women, potential victims, fall prey to absence, silence, and madness." . . .

[Writer] Susan Griffin argues that "more than rape itself, the fear of rape permeates our lives . . . and the best defense against this is not to be, to deny being in the body, as a self; . . . to avert your gaze, make yourself, as a presence in this world, less felt." Certainly, when Celie speaks of turning herself into wood when she is beaten or raped ("I say to myself, Celie, you a tree"), the response described by Griffin is apparent; to avoid pain Celie denies her body and her presence. Walker's story begins in the familiar mythic way: Celie is told after her rape by her (presumed) father: "*You better not never tell nobody but God. It'd kill your mammy.*" Celie is silenced by an external source, and like Morrison's and Naylor's protagonists, she experiences the nullification of subjectivity and internal voice allied with rape by the myth of Philomela. Celie's story starts with the fact that the one identity she has always known is no longer accessible: "I am fourteen years old. I have always been a good girl." No longer a "good girl," Celia has no present tense subjectivity, no present tense "I am."

Bird and Blood Become Symbols of Rebirth

Like Pecola Breedlove of Morrison's *The Bluest Eye*, who ends the novel "flail[ing] her arms like a bird in an eternal, grotesquely futile effort to fly," Celie appears to have been driven into semiotic [symbolic] collapse by the rape. Walker's text also uses bird and blood imagery to connect Celie with her mythic prototype, Philomela as well as to revise the mythic prototext. In [his narrative poem] *Metamorphoses*, Ovid describes how Procne and Philomela are transformed, a change that silences them as humans but does not erase their bloody deeds: "One flew to the woods, the other to the roof-top, / And even so the red marks of the murder / Stayed on their breasts; the feathers were blood-colored." Throughout *The Color Purple*, Celie is associated with both birds and blood. Celie tells Albert that she loves birds, and Albert comments, "you use to remind me of a bird. Way back when you first come to live with me. . . . And the least little thing happen, you looked about to fly away." Later in the novel, when Celie

The symbols in Alice Walker's novel The Color Purple *connect her character Celie with the Greek myth of Philomela (pictured). Philomela was raped and forced into silence.* © Mary Evans Picture Library/Alamy.

returns to confront her "Pa" (Alphonso) about his actions, she comments three times on how loudly the birds are singing around his house. The singing birds of the later scene recall Celie's earlier victimization, the way she was raped, bloodied, impregnated, and deprived of voice by Alphonso's statement that "she tell lies."

Paradoxically, the birds of this scene are also a positive symbol to Celie of how nature persists in displaying its beauty despite the despoiling patterns of humanity. Similarly, Walker later transforms the blood symbolism of the early rape scene ("Seem like it all come back to me. . . . How the blood drip down my leg and mess up my stocking") into something more positive, revising the symbolism of blood in the mythic text. When Shug abandons Celie, Celie describes her heart as "blooming blood." Here, although blood is painful, it is also generative: it blooms. Blood comes from Celie during her rape. It also covers her in other key scenes in the novel, such as her first meeting with Mr.——'s (Albert's) family: "I spend my wedding day running from the oldest boy. . . . He pick up a rock and laid my head open. The blood run all down tween my breasts." Like Philomela, whose breast feathers are stained "blood-colored" with the "red marks of the murder" after she is transformed into a bird, Celie's breasts are stained with blood. However, Celie eventually transforms the blood of this attack into blooming blood, into a red that is creative and regenerative. A more mature Celie uses the color red as a positive element in her sewing, transforming it from a color of pain to a color of joy. She sews purple and red pants for Sofia, orange and red pants for Squeak, and blue and red pants for Shug. She paints her own room purple and red. The blood that marks Celie becomes a positive symbol of her artistic creativity, rather than (as in the myth) a negative symbol of how she is damned in perpetuity by her deed.

Celie Finds Power in Her Voice

Unlike the archetypal narrative, then, Walker's novel uses bird and blood imagery to suggest Celie's metamorphosis not from human to subhuman, but from victim to artist-heroine. The novel also differs from the mythic prototext, as well as from the novels of Morrison and Naylor, in that it begins (rather than ends) with Celie's rape, and in that the rape becomes not an instrument of silencing, but the catalyst to Celie's search for voice. After Celie is told to be silent about the rape, she confides the details in her journal, structured at first as letters to God. In these letters Celie begins to create a resistant narratological version of events that ultimately preserves her subjectivity and voice. . . .

The horror of this experience is evident, but it is also apparent that Celie narrates these events to *resist* her father. Susan Brownmiller comments that "Rape by an authority figure can befuddle a victim. . . . Authority figures emanate an aura of rightness; their actions cannot easily be challenged. What else can the victim be but 'wrong'"? . . .

Celie's movement out of silence occurs despite repeated rape by her husband, who in his demeanor and behavior exactly parallels her father. Multiple or repeated rape is an important element of the violation detailed in the archetypal myth of Philomela as well as in texts by contemporary African American women. In the mythic text, after Tereus cuts out Philomela's tongue he rapes her again, perhaps more than once: "And even then—/ It seems too much to believe—even then, Tereus / Took her, and took her again, the injured body / Still giving satisfaction to his lust". . . .

Celie, too, is repeatedly raped by her "Pa," who impregnates her twice and then gives away her children. Celie is also raped, both actually and symbolically, by her husband, Mr.——(or Albert). Celie is quick to note the parallels between her husband and her father: "Mr.——say. . . . All women good for—he don't finish. He just tuck his chin over the paper like he do. Remind me of Pa." And Celie's letters repeatedly emphasis that sex with Albert is the equivalent of rape. . . .

Finding Herself in Writing Letters

Walker's title may be an allusion to Philomela's text, woven in purple. However, in Ovid's myth this alternative text leads only to Philomela's further victimization by Tereus and to her silence. Celie, too, finds an alternative text, a text directed at a non-patriarchal audience, for in the second half of the novel she stops writing to God—whom she perceives as "just like all the other mens I know. Trifling, forgitful and lowdown"—and starts writing to Nettie.

While Philomela's alternative text leads to her destruction, Celie's alternative text, her letters to Nettie, leads to reconstruction, allowing Celie to craft an identity for herself as the heroine of her own story. Celie gets a house and a profession, and she describes both these events in heroic terms in her letters to Nettie. Both Procne and Philomela are taken away from their familial homes by Tereus. Similarly, both Nettie and Celie are driven away from their family's home by the individual they call "Pa." Unlike Procne and Philomela, both Celie and Nettie return. Celie's letter to Nettie describes her triumphant homecoming and ends with the statement that "Now you [Nettie] can come home cause you have a home to come to!" Signing this letter "Your loving sister, Celie," Celie asserts both her right to this home and to this text in which she is no longer a displaced wife trapped within a patriarchal plot. Although Celie seldom signs her letters, she also signs the letter in which she describes her new profession to Nettie. These two signatures, "Your loving Sister, Celie," and "Your Sister, Celie, Folkspants, Unlimited" indicate the contours of the heroic role Celie has shaped for herself, and contrast sharply with her earlier inability to say "I am." And only in the second half of the novel, when Celie stops writing to God and starts writing to Nettie, does she actively articulate an alternative identity for herself. . . .

Language as a Tool, Not a Weapon

In the mythic pattern, Tereus doubly silences Philomela, first by pulling out her tongue and then by imprisoning her in a tower, just as Albert doubly silences Celie, denying her voice ("you can't curse nobody") and presence ("I should have lock you up"). But Celie silences and imprisons the oppressor within her own narrative: "the jail you plan for me is the one in which you will rot," "You better stop talking." Like Albert, Celie has learned how to use both physical and linguistic violence to erase others.

However, Walker is not content with showing Celie's use of "the master's tools" against the master. Celie must learn that language can be used to understand, rather than destroy.

Walker Revises Traditional Gender Roles

Mae G. Henderson

Mae G. Henderson is professor of English and comparative literature at the University of North Carolina at Chapel Hill. She has authored articles and essays on subjects such as African American and feminist literary criticism and theory, pedagogy, theater, and diaspora and cultural studies. She has edited various books, including Borders, Boundaries, and Frames *(1995).*

In this selection, Henderson concentrates on the radical changes, especially with regard to gender, in the lives of the African American characters in The Color Purple. *Some of the women in the novel (Celie's mother is an exception) sacrifice for one another from the beginning, protecting each other from male cruelty, asserts Henderson. The women are the ones to reform and heal relationships and values of the world in which they must live. Celie and Squeak are the more subservient women at first, claims Henderson, and Shug and Sophia the defiant ones. They comprise a large network of women who bond with each other, share their responsibilities, and challenge the prevailing hierarchy based on race and gender. In Henderson's view,* The Color Purple *examines the patriarchal culture among black people in both North America and Africa, where women are mistreated by controlling men. In the novel, Henderson concludes, the abusive traditional family is finally replaced by an extended family in which male and female roles are reversed.*

Mae G. Henderson, "*The Color Purple*: Revisions and Redefinitions," *Sage: A Scholarly Journal on Black Women*, vol. 2, Spring 1985. Copyright © 1985 Sage: A Scholarly Journal on Black Women. Expanded and reprinted under the title "Alice Walker's The Color Purple: Revisions and Redefinitions" in Harold Bloom (Ed.) *Modern Critical Views: Alice Walker* (New York, Chelsea House, 1989). All rights reserved. Reproduced by permission of the author.

The Color Purple is a novel which deals with what it means to be poor, black, and female in the rural South during the first half of the twentieth century. In an interview in *Newsweek* in June 1982, [Alice] Walker explains that Celie, the protagonist of *The Color Purple*, is modeled after the author's own grandmother, who was raped at the age of twelve by her slave owner (and Walker's grandfather). Celie's fate, however, is brighter. "I liberated her from her own history," remarks Walker, "I wanted her to be happy." Walker hopes that "people can hear Celie's voice. There are so many people like Celie who make it, who came out of nothing. People who triumphed." Thus, for Walker, art is liberational and life-saving; it is an act for reconstruction and reclamation of self, of past, of women, and of community. . . .

The Values of Slavery Suppress Black Women

The arrival of Mister represents an ironic reversal of the fairy tale in which the steed-mounted knight in shining armor arrives to save the damsel in distress. Resonating through this passage, however, are not the chimes of medieval chivalry, but the echo of the slavers' auction block in the sale and bartering of a human commodity in a quasi-feudal Southern economy. Celie's status as slave, or chattel property—subservient to father and later to husband (and to God)—expected to perform domestic, field, and sexual labor, is confirmed when Albert is assured that the "cow [is] coming."

The inscription of slavery is critical to understanding Walker's intentions. If Mister has inherited from his father, Old Mister, the farm which belonged to his grandfather, the white slaveowner, he has likewise inherited from Old Mister the values of ownership, mastery, and domination bequeathed by the white slaveowner. These values, he attempts, in turn, to impose on his own son, Harpo. For Walker, it is the institution of slavery and its legacy which are largely responsible for setting into motion the oppressive mode characterizing relations between men and women, white and black, powerful and powerless. . . .

The model for the patriarchal scheme in the novel has already been established by Albert's father, who has dissuaded his son from marrying the only woman he has ever loved, Shug Avery ("She black as tar, she nappy headed. She got legs like baseball bats"). Like his father before him, Albert attempts to prevent his own son from marrying Sofia, the woman of his choice and the mother of his child: "No need to think I'm gon let my boy marry you just cause you in the family way. He young and limited. Pretty gal like you could put anything over on him." Although Harpo, in defiance of his father, finally does bring home Sofia and his baby, he tries to beat her just as his father beats Celie. . . .

Celie Brainwashed to Accept Patriarchy

Over and over again, Celie accepts abuse and victimization. When Harpo asks her what to do to "make [Sofia] mind," Celie, having internalized the principle of male domination, answers, "Beat her." When Celie next sees Harpo, "his face [is] a mess of bruises." Sofia, then, becomes Celie's first model of resistance to sexual, and later, racial subjugation. Cheeky and rebellious, Sofia is described as an "amazon" of a woman. She scorns rigid gender definitions and prefers fixing the leaking roof to fixing the evening dinner. Moreover, as Harpo quickly learns, Sofia gives as well as she takes. "All my life I had to fight," Sofia explains to Celie, "I had to fight my daddy. I had to fight my brothers. I had to fight my cousins and my uncles. A girl child ain't safe in a family of men." Not only does Sofia resist Harpo's attempts to impose submission, she is also jailed for "sassing" the mayor's wife and knocking the mayor down when he slaps her for impudence.

Unlike Sofia, however, Celie submits to a system of beliefs and values which reinforce conventional notions of race, class, and sex—and relegate her to a subordinate status. Celie submits to male authority because she accepts a theology which requires female subjugation to father and husband. Having been taught to "honor father and mother no matter what," Celie "couldn't be mad at [her] daddy because he [her] daddy." She suffers Albert's abuse for the same reasons: "Well, sometime Mr.———git on me pretty hard. I have to talk to Old Maker. But he my husband, I shrug my shoulders." . . .

Transforming the Patriarchal Scheme

If her body has been devalued by the men in her life, Celie not only discovers her own sexuality in the relationship with Shug, but she also learns how to love another. The recognition of herself as beautiful, and loving is the first step towards Celie's independence and self-acceptance. If Celie, however, becomes more self-reliant, Shug becomes more nurturing and caring. In the course of the friendship, both women are transformed.

Unlike Celie, who derives her sense of self from the dominant white and male theology, Shug is a self-invented character whose sense of self is not male-inscribed. Her theology allows a divine, self-authorized sense of self. Shug's conception of God is both imminent and transcendent:

> God inside you and inside everybody else. You come into the world with God. But only them that search for it inside find it. And sometimes it just manifest itself even if you not looking, or don't know what you looking for. . . . I believe God is everything. . . . Everything that is or ever was or ever will be.

Shug rejects the scriptural notion of God: "Ain't no way to read the bible and not think God white. . . . When I found out I thought God was white, and a man, I lost interest." Describing her god as "it," Shug explains that "god ain't a he or a she." God, for Shug, is not only someone to please, but to be pleased: "I think it pisses God off if you walk by the color purple in a field somewhere and don't notice it."

Celie begins to revise her own notions of God and man and her place within the scheme of patriarchy when she discovers, through the agency of Shug, the cache of letters which Albert has concealed from her. Not only does she discover that her sister and children are in Africa, perhaps separated from her forever, but that her real father had been lynched and her mother driven mad. These calamities and misfortunes shatter Celie's faith in the "big. . . old. . . tall. . . graybearded" white man to whom she has been "praying and writing." "He act just like all the other mens I know," writes Celie, "trifling, forgetful, and lowdown." Resisting the authority of a patriarchal god as well as that of her husband, Celie learns to assert herself both in writing and speaking. When she recognizes that "the god [she] has been writing to is a man" who does not listen to "poor colored women," she begins to address her letters to sister Nettie.

Writing thus becomes, for Celie, a means of structuring her identity—her sense of self—in relationship to her sister, and by extension, a community of women. The subsequent letters between Celie and Nettie stand as a profound affirmation of the creative and self-creative power of the word. Because the letters, due to Albert's expropriation, are never answered, it is apparent that they function primarily for the benefit of the writers, rather than the recipients. The dedication of the book ("*To the Spirit*: Without whose assistance / Neither this book / Nor I / Would have been / Written") suggests that to create a book is to create a life. Celie (like her creator, Walker) writes herself and her story into being. Moreover, the transformation of the letters represents and parallels, to some extent, the growth and change in the lives of the writers. Not only do Nettie's letters become more formal and didactic in style as she is educated in the manners and mores of the Olinka tribe, but Celie's letters become longer and more sophisticated as she articulates a more reflective and complex sense of self. The correspondence between Celie and Nettie attests to the power of literacy and, at the same time, reinforces the motifs of community and female bonding that underlines the novel.

Celie's defiance of Albert is both a mark of increasing literacy, as well as a milestone in her journey toward maturity and independence. . . .

Women Degraded in Africa and the American South

If Celie is degraded and devalued as a black woman in the American South, Nettie discovers that, as an unmarried female, she is regarded with pity and contempt by the Olinka. She also learns about scarification and clitoridectomy, rituals of female mutilation in a patriarchal society. Tashi, the young Olinka woman whom Celie's son marries, submits to both these rites in order to preserve some vestige of tribal culture and identity in the face of white encroachment upon traditional village life. Tashi's choice suggests, of course, the conflict between the demands of race and the demands of sex confronting black women. With these rituals, black patriarchal culture replicates the historic occidental relationship between whites and blacks. Scarification and clitoridectomy both externalize the historic victimization of black women and symbolize gender debasement in patriarchal culture.

In Africa, however, Nettie discovers among the Olinka the value of female bonding in a polygynous society. "It is in work that women get to know and care about each other," she writes to Celie. Moreover, in the missionary household where she lives with Samuel, a black minister, and his wife, Corrine, Nettie shares the responsibility of rearing the children and administers to the spiritual and medical needs of the Olinka.

Yet, it is Celie and Shug who epitomize the complementarity as well as the autonomy of the women—which extend to include not only other women, but also the men. While developing an individual sense of self, Celie nevertheless respects Shug's rights. Although heartbroken that Shug has run off with Germaine, a young musician in her band, Celie recognizes that "[Shug] got a right to look over the world in whatever company she choose. Just cause I love her don't take away none of her rights. . . . Who am I to tell her who to love? My job just to love her good and true myself." Albert's feelings for Shug, together with his desertion by Shug and Celie, constitute the catalyst for a similar recognition in his life: "I have love and I have been love. And I thank God he let me gain understanding enough to know love can't be halted just cause some peoples moan and groan. It don't surprise me you [Celie] love Shug Avery. . . . I have love Shug Avery all my life." Finding consolation in each other's company, Albert and Celie become friends for the first time, and spend their evenings sharing interests and reminiscing about Shug.

A Revision of Gender Roles

By the end of the novel, we see that Walker has developed a new model for relationships based on new gender roles for men and women. Not only do Albert and Harpo extend their interests to include activities such as sewing and cooking but, perhaps more importantly, they begin to relate more affectively to each other. When Albert is nearly dying, Harpo bathes and nurtures his father back to health. Walker suggests here that less rigid and oppressive roles are necessary in order for men and women to live together and fulfill their individual potential. Celie's notions of "manliness" and "womanliness" challenge rigid gender categories and allow for individual variations and preferences:

> Mr.———ast me the other day what it is I love so much
> bout Shug. He say he love her style. He say, to tell the truth,
> Shug act more *manly* than most men. I mean she upright,
> honest. Speak her mind and the devil take the hindmost, he

say. You know Shug will fight, he say. Just like Sofia. She bound to live her life and be herself no matter what.

Mr.———think all this is stuff men do. But Harpo not like this, I tell him. You not like this. What Shug got is *womanly* it seem like to me. Specially since she and Sofia the ones got it [Emphasis added.]

Walker not only redefines male and female roles, she also suggests a new paradigm for relationships. During the course of the novel, Shug leaves Albert and returns married to Grady, "a skinny big toof man." She later runs off with the youthful Germaine. The intimacy between Celie and Shug, however, survives and incorporates each of these relationships.

In Memphis, the initial triad of Shug, Celie, and Albert gives way to a triad consisting of Celie, Shug, and Grady (or alternately, Squeak, Shug, and Grady). When Shug takes up with Germaine, a new triad develops—Celie, Shug, and Germaine. Other triads in the novel include Squeak, Harpo, and Sofia and Nettie, Corrine, and Samuel. The final triad in the novel, formed when Shug returns to Celie, is, in fact, a reconstitution of the first—Shug, Celie, and Albert—with *radically redefined roles.*

Women Support a New Family Network

Walker's final paradigm, then, is neither the male/female nor the female/female dyad, but a variation on the eternal triangle in which women complement rather than compete with each other, and at the same time, share an equal status with the men. Thus, the novel moves from a male/female coupling in which the woman is subjugated, to a female/female coupling based on mutuality, to a female/male/female triad based on new and redefined roles. In Walker's new model, conventional heterosexual relationships and nuclear families give way to a triad which radiates outwards into an extended family network linked by women. Walker's paradigm is confirmed by the work of contemporary feminist scholars such as Nancy Chodorow and Elizabeth Abel who hold that primary bonding exists between women. Moreover, like Chodorow, Walker's resolution to sexual inequality depends on fostering an increased sense of male self-in-relationship and a greater sense of female autonomy. If Harpo learns to "mother" his father, Celie learns to earn her own livelihood. Walker's women, through their unconventional lifestyles, gain greater access to the public sphere. (Celie replaces her real father as owner of a dry-goods store, while both Shug and Squeak, as blues singers, perform in public. Both Harpo and Albert, on the other hand, in their enjoyment of cooking and sewing, as well as their heightened sense of nurturance and connectedness, move further into the private or domestic arena.)

The novel ends on a theme of reunion between lovers, family, and friends, symbolizing on a personal level, the psychic reintegration of personality differences and on a social level, the reconciliation of gender differences. Having enrolled Germaine in Wilberforce, Shug returns to join Celie, now the successful owner of a house and business, and Albert, who is content to sit back and learn "to wonder." Finally, drawing again on the conventions of the sentimental novel, Celie is reunited with her two children who have returned with her long-lost sister from Africa.

Trading Male Literary Traditions for Female Oral Ones

Valerie Babb

A professor of English at the University of Georgia, Valerie Babb is also an author whose writings include Whiteness Visible.

In this article, Babb argues that the cultural split that has given whites dominance over blacks and men over women—plus the fact that literacy and the writing of literature have been the traditional prerogatives of white males—has been a social tool to deny black women writers the tools of power. Woman's primacy, she states, is the oral tradition. Such is the case of Celie. According to Babb, in a novel composed of letters written in the oral tradition, in dialect, the traditional hierarchy is eventually turned on its head. The black males are overcome by the black women, and the oral tradition of a black woman becomes more important and stronger than the white male's written tradition. Another aspect of the cultural divide, says Babb, is the concept of God. At first, Celie addresses a white, male God, but she comes to abandon that image as she addresses her letters to her sister, Nettie, shifting to a caring audience before finding her own all-inclusive God. Nettie also uses written literary tradition to preserve the African oral one.

The Color Purple is not only a novel in which black women make an inhospitable male environment amenable to their growth and development, it is also an epistolary novel in which black women take a form traditionally inhospitable to oral cultures, the written word, and transform it, making it,

Valerie Babb, "*The Color Purple*: Writing to Undo What Writing Has Done," *Phylon: The Atlanta University Review of Race and Culture*, vol. XLVII/2, Summer 1986. Copyright © 1986 by Phylon: The Atlanta University Review of Race and Culture. Reproduced by permission.

too, responsive to their needs. The society in which Alice Walker places her main characters, Celie and Nettie, is the result of specific historical events and cultural values which placed whites in a dominant position over blacks, men in a dominant position over women, and most important for the purposes of this paper, literacy in a dominant position over oral expression. What Alice Walker effects in *The Color Purple* is a reorganization of this hierarchy, so that blacks may minimize their oppression by whites, women may free themselves from the dominance of males, and oral expression is no longer subjugated by written expression.

Black Women Writers Using White Male Literary Devices

The epistolary form of this novel itself calls attention to the act of writing by using letters to construct a tale. Once aware of the conspicuous presence of writing, we cannot help but note that a transformation occurs in terms of both its function and form. In the first half of the work, Celie uses writing to effect self-actualization, and its standard form is modified as elements of the oral are injected into it. In the second half of the novel, Nettie uses writing to record the oral history of Africa and Afro-Americans, and its function as a cultural element whose appearance generally signals the disappearance of the oral is altered. Thus, within this novel, two black women employ a device traditionally used by a white male culture to ensure its authority....

In Walker's novel, both Celie and Nettie learn to master the written word and to modify its form and function so that they, as black women, are no longer complete victims of the racial and sexual oppression a white, ethnocentric use of writing can dictate. By mastering and modifying writing, Celie and Nettie change it into an implement that is no longer

Alice Walker places Celie and her sister, Nettie (pictured in a scene from the film The Color Purple*), in a white-dominated society.* © Photos 12/Alamy.

solely the property of men and whites, but one used by black women to gain a greater awareness of themselves and to preserve their oral history.

The Culture's Writing and God Are White and Male

The novel opens, with the fourteen-year-old Celie's first letter to God, in which she asks him to tell her why the man she believes is her father (but who is actually her stepfather) repeatedly rapes her, impregnates her twice, and takes from her the two children she has borne. That Celie writes to a God she envisions as white and male indicates the thoroughness with which whites and men have asserted their dominant position in her mind. It is her stepfather who tells her, "*You better not never tell nobody but God. It'd kill your mammy.*" That she writes out of desperation shows that literacy has accompanied this dominance, supplanting the role of the oral. Since writing can be a tool of racial and sexual dominance, it is not surprising that Celie perceives it as she does God, all-powerful, and feels it is the only form of expression which is able to alleviate her confusion and shame.

When Celie's stepfather marries her to Albert, a man who views her as a brute convenience, and when Albert forces the separation of Celie from her sister, Nettie, the only person she feels truly loves her, Celie continues to record her feelings in the form of letters to God. Several years later, with the aid of her female friend and subsequent lover, Shug Avery, Celie discovers Albert has kept Nettie's letters from her. The letters record Nettie's thoughts and experiences as she is separated from Celie, is employed by a missionary minister and his wife, and journeys to Africa with them as a missionary herself. By not receiving the letters, Celie not only loses contact with her sister, but also loses a valuable opportunity for cultural education.

Although the sisters lead very separate and different lives, writing is important to each of them. The more Celie writes, the more she is able to analyze her experience and subsequently herself. She uses writing to fix the events of her life, thereby lending them coherence and making their review and understanding possible. Like Celie, Nettie, too, feels compelled to place her experience in written form, so that she may gain a greater awareness of her consciousness; while Nettie does this, however, she also records the larger experience of Afro-America, giving it the tangibility of a written text, so that its oral history is not lost.

Using Literacy to Escape Male Oppression

That both sisters choose to write is a direct result of their being imprisoned in a male-dominated, literacy-oriented culture where men arrange their marriages, and men decide how much access they will have to the written word. Though the most evident male dominance in the sisters' world takes a sexual form, overtones of literacy as an element of power are present. When motivated by sexually selfish desires, their step-father makes the following transparent excuse to a prospective suitor, "I can't let you have Nettie. . . . I want her to git some more schooling. . . . But I can let you have Celie." Here her stepfather shows that he not only has the power to barter them into marriage, but should he choose, also the power to decide on the availability of literacy to them.

The power of literacy to provide an escape from sexual subjugation is also evident as illustrated by the events follow-ing Celie's rape. When Nettie seems to be next in line for the same violation, Celie vows to protect her sister, and realizes the best way to do so is to ensure that Nettie has power, the power of literacy: "I see him looking at my little sister. She scared. . . . But I say I'll take care of you. . . . I tell Nettie to keep at her books." . . .

Shifting to an Audience That Cares

Perhaps the most telling effect of Celie's making the written form responsive to her needs is her shifting choice of audi-ence. Realizing God has been indifferent to her writing, she now addresses an audience she know cares, her sister:

> Dear Nettie,
>
> I don't write to God no more, I write to you. . . . [T]he God I been praying and writing to is a man. And act just like all the other mens I know. Trifling, forgitful and lowdown. . . . If he ever listened to poor colored women the world would be a different place. . . .

By imbuing written words with her own oral forms, Celie cre-ates a new literacy which enables her to explore her own con-sciousness, create a new world vision, and even question the role God plays in her life. No longer is she isolated, writing only to a male God who does not heed her. She has found a human audience in her sister, and a holistic universal audience in the trees, stars and sky. Now viewing God not as a man, but as a presence found in many places including natural elements, she is even able to include God in her audience, and she writes to everything: "Dear God. Dear stars, dear trees, dear sky, dear peoples. Dear Everything. Dear God."

It is important to note here that Celie's heightened consciousness and self-awareness grows out of a coupling of her own written expression and the reading of Nettie's letters. Upon their discovery and after Shug places the letters in temporal order for Celie, the cohesion and order Celie seeks in her life begin to take form. In her letters, Nettie draws on their shared early experiences, adds them to her own in Africa, and formulates a new text for them both. She too alters literacy and takes it out of its imperialistic function of dominating oral cultures and allows it to record an oral history that would otherwise be lost. . . .

Celie and Nettie Preserve African and African American Oral Culture

As much as documenting African life, Nettie's record also preserves the links which join African culture to Afro-American culture. Her description of an interchange between Tashi, a child of the village, and Olivia, actually Celie's daughter, as they recall oral tales is an example:

> Sometimes Tashi comes over and tells stories that are popular among the Olinka children. I am encouraging her and Olivia to write them down in Olinka and English. . . . Olivia feels that, compared to Tashi, she has no good stories to tell. One day she started in on an "Uncle Remus" tale only to discover Tashi had the original version of it! . . . But then we got into a discussion of how Tashi's people's stories got to America. . . .

Nettie has thus used writing to do exactly what it has not done in the past, preserve rather than destroy oral culture. In this instance, she has also encouraged her charges, members of a new generation, to do the same, thus attempting the continuity of oral history.

In the experiences of both Celie and Nettie, then, we see writing transformed. Working within a culture that is literacy-oriented, where, as [Swiss linguist] Ferdinand de Saussure notes, "Most people pay more attention to visual impressions simply because these are sharper and more lasting than aural impressions ... ," the sisters revise and reuse writing. No longer is it an oppressive implement, for Celie transforms it into the instrument that will end the male-oppressiveness of her world. No longer is it antagonistic to oral expression, for Nettie uses it for the preservation of oral culture.

For most of *The Color Purple* neither sister receives the other's letters. The capacity of writing as a communicative link is thus overshadowed by its capacity to lend stasis to human experience so that it can be assessed and its capacity for recording and creating permanent history. When Celie and Nettie's letters reach each other and are looked at as a unified body, they, and thus the novel, echo the larger themes that are part of Afro-American history. The cycle of rape or attempted rape, oppression, escape, and awareness that each sister becomes a part of is a smaller representation of these elements within the course of black history: rape, manifested when blacks were forcibly taken from their home land; oppression, manifested when blacks were enslaved and treated as second-class citizens; escape, manifested as blacks sought avenues out of enslavement and eventual emancipation; and awareness, manifested in a growing black pride in African ancestry.

While telling the story of two sisters, Walker has also told the story of African, Afro-American, and Afro-American female experience. In *The Color Purple* she has created a unique monument to these sagas, as her characters take the written form which ignored Afro-American history and culture and use it to preserve both.

Walker's Relationship with the African American Male

Philip M. Royster

Philip M. Royster, a professor of English at Kansas State University for many years and now director of the African American Cultural Center at the University of Illinois–Chicago, has published books of his poetry and articles on writers Langston Hughes, Toni Morrison, and Alice Walker.

In this essay Royster discusses how The Color Purple *has been at the center of controversy, chiefly over Alice Walker's characterization of black men and women and their relationship to one another. On one hand, says Royster, the novel has been compared with the those of the renowned American author William Faulkner. On the other, it has been derided for its stereotypes: violent black men and helpless, acquiescent women. Walker has stated in interviews that her role is to liberate black women, to rescue them from the black male's exploitation of women. Yet, Royster claims, Walker is considered to have alienated both black men and black women in her audience. Questions are continually raised about the novel's relationship to the exploiters and the oppressed in the culture she creates. Royster contends that Walker's attempt to be a rescuer fails because of stereotypes.*

Alice Walker's third novel, *The Color Purple*, is fueling controversy in many black American communities. Afro-American novelist/critic David Bradley recalls "sens[ing] that *The Color Purple* was going to be ground zero at a Hiroshima of controversy." Some women have found it difficult to lay the book down unfinished; some men have bellowed with rage while reading it (as well as afterwards). It appears that Walker's

Philip M. Royster, "In Search of Our Father's Arms: Alice Walker's Persona of the Alienated Darling," *Black American Literature Forum*, vol. 20, Winter 1986. Copyright © 1986 by Black American Literature Forum. Reproduced by permission.

depiction of violent black men who physically and psychologically abuse their wives and children is one of the poles of the controversy and that her depiction of lesbianism is another.

Critical Controversy over Gender

Many critics have praised the novel, especially for its use of a black dialect that reviewers laud in such terms as "positively poetic," "eloquent," and "masterful." A reviewer in the *New Yorker* labeled the novel "fiction of the highest order." [Critic] Peter Prescott called it "an American novel of permanent importance." A *Publishers Weekly* reviewer considers the book "stunning and brilliantly conceived"; [Critic] Mel Watkins regards the novel as "striking and consummately well-written"; and [author and critic] Dinitia Smith believes that "at least half the book is superb, it places . . . [Walker] in the company of Faulkner."

Yet, not all of those who have read the novel have liked it, including many black women. Bradley observes that "one black poet, Sonia Sanchez, criticized Alice Walker's theme of black male brutality as an overemphasis. Another black woman told me 'The Color Purple' was 'a begging kind of piece' and she was 'getting tired of being beat over the head with this women's lib stuff, and this whole black woman/black man, "Lord have mercy on us po' sisters," kind of thing' in Alice Walker's work." One of the strongest responses to the novel has come from [literary scholar] Trudier Harris, who believes the novel should be ignored because of its portrayal of a protagonist that is not merely idiosyncratic but unrealistic, and because the book's portrayal of domestic violence is based on unwholesome stereotypes of black folk and their communities that appeal to spectator readers.

This polarization of responses to *The Color Purple* may be better understood by focusing attention on Walker's expressed fictive and nonfictive attitudes towards her role as a writer, her intended audience, and the issues of sexuality and aggression.

The Writer as Alienated Rescuer

Walker has committed her efforts to at least two great social movements that have stimulated the alteration of consciousness in the last half of the twentieth century: the Civil Rights Movement and the Women's Liberation Movement. Walker's involvement with these movements both generates and reflects her intention, first articulated in 1973, to champion as a writer the causes of black people, especially black women: "I am preoccupied with the spiritual survival, the survival *whole*, of my people. But beyond that, I am committed to exploring the oppressions, the insanities, the loyalties, and the triumphs of black women."

In a 1984 interview, Walker revealed that, since childhood, she has seen herself as a writer who rescues: "'I was brought up to try to see what was wrong and right it. Since I am a writer, writing is how I right it.'" Walker's fiction confronts such issues as racism, intraracism, sexism, neocolonialism, and imperialism in order to transform both society and the individual. She expressed her commitment to change in 1973 with the affirmation: "I believe in change: change personal, and change in society." In *The Color Purple*, she seems to be preoccupied with the task of overcoming black male sexist exploitation of black women. . . .

The Writer's Audience

The issue of audience identification is especially important in a multi-cultural society in which one culture creates institutions that exploit, manipulate, and dominate other cultures. What a writer understands of her own relationships to the dialectical tensions between the exploiter and the exploited, the oppressor and the oppressed, or the persecutor and the victim is important. Does the writer see herself as the rescuer or champion of the exploited, uncontaminated herself by oppression or oppressive values; does she regard herself as being involved in the circle of the victims; or is she drawn unwittingly into the circle of the persecutors? [Psychiatrist and philosopher] Frantz Fanon articulates some of the issues for the "native intellectual" struggling with the influence of the "colonial bourgeoisie" in *The Wretched of the Earth*. These issues influence the writer's fictive and nonfictive voices and the reader's interpretations of the writer's texts, so despite the pitfalls yawning as one leaps from a writer's recorded assertions and perceptions to a theory for understanding that writer's fiction, it is urgent to examine Walker's attitudes towards her audience. Moreover, examining her written perceptions of and attitudes towards her past experiences allows one to better understand her handling of the concepts of sexuality and aggression. It permits the critic to create a bridge of understanding that joins the writer, with her work, to more of her readers.

If Walker's intention in writing *The Color Purple* was to lessen the oppression of black women by black men, a reasonable question is: To whom is the work directed—black men, black women, or both? Who is going to be responsible for ending sexist exploitation, and who is going to determine the means to that end? Walker's reaction to criticism of *The Color Purple* reveals that she is not satisfied with the responses from at least one segment of her audience: "'I just always expected people to understand. Black men, because of their oppression, I always thought, would understand. So the criticism that I have had from black men, especially, who don't want me to write about these things, I'm just amazed.'" Walker's disappointment with criticism by black men suggests that she intends for them to be sitting in the audience before her stage waiting to be moved by her performance. Also, they could be looking over her shoulder to provide critical direction and approval as she writes. Whether or not black males make up both stage and critical audiences, a discrepancy exists between authorial intention and audience reaction. My work with Alice Walker's writings suggests that her recorded attitudes towards segments of her intended audience make it difficult for her to communicate effectively with them. . . .

Visions of the Missions of Black Women

After considering Alice Walker's assertions of alienation from black people, it is indeed ironic to examine her approval, in 1971, of [author, activist, and widow of Martin Luther King Jr.] Coretta King's vision that black women who feel compassion, love justice, and have resisted embitterment will become leaders of mankind. Walker says of Mrs. King:

> . . . she says something that I feel is particularly true: "Women, in general, are not a part of the corruption of the past, so they can give a new kind of leadership, a new image for mankind. But if they are going to be bitter or vindictive they are not going to be able to do this. But they're capable of tremendous compassion, love, and forgiveness, which if they use it, can make this a better world. When you think of what some black women have gone through, and then look at how beautiful they still are! It is incredible that they still believe in the values of the race, that they have retained a love of justice, that they can still feel the deepest compassion, not only for themselves but for anybody who is oppressed; this is a kind of miracle, something we have that we must preserve and pass on."

Coretta King is drawing a picture of a female rescuer of the race who is adequate for her role; that is, one who maintains it without switching to the roles of either victim or persecutor. Although Walker admires the image, she does not appear to be cut of that cloth. King might be speaking indirectly of her perceptions of Walker, challenging the writer to rise above them.

But Walker does not use King's ideal to measure herself; rather, she challenges the ideal with her own feminist concern:

"I want to know her opinion of why black women have been antagonistic toward women's liberation. As a black woman myself, I say, I do not understand this because black women among all women have been oppressed almost beyond recognition—oppressed by *everyone*." Walker's complaint suggests that she perceives a psychic distance between herself and the community of black women, who, generally speaking (and this was even more true in 1971), are unwilling to join a white women's movement. Walker's emotional generalization that everyone oppresses black women, one of her hobbyhorses, is an exaggeration that reflects her alienation: Accustomed to viewing herself as an outcast, Walker here places black women generally in opposition to everyone else. . . .

Criticism of Walker's Feminist Stance

On the other hand, in 1984, when David Bradley criticized her for failing to be as tough on black women as on black men, Walker responded not merely by excusing black women's weaknesses but also by arguing that the motives of women are less reprehensible than those of men: "'But I am really aware that they are under two layers of oppression and that even though everybody, the men and the women, get [sic] twisted terribly, the women have less choice than the men. And the things that they do, the bad choices that they make, are not done out of meanness, out of a need to take stuff out on people.'" The persona is clever enough to reach for feminist rhetoric, "two layers of oppression" (as if black men have not been and are not still sexually and racially exploited by black women and white people), but she destroys the credibility of her position with feminist (or would this be womanist?) psychology: the assertion of gender-determined meanness. . . .

Negative View of Men Since Childhood

Undoubtedly, Walker's alienation from black men influences her portrayal of them in fiction. Her audiences may achieve greater tolerance of her perceptions of men if they consider

Walker's portrayal of male characters as part of the aftermath of the childhood accident in which she was blinded in one eye after her brother shot her with a bb gun. David Bradley asserts that "after that accident, she felt her family had failed her, especially her father. She felt he had ceased to favor her, and, as a child, blamed him for the poverty that kept her from receiving adequate medical care. He also, she implies, whipped and imprisoned her sister, who had shown too much interest in boys. . . . In company with her brothers, her father had failed to 'give me male models I could respect.'" Walker's disenchantment sounds like that of a child who no longer feels like her father's darling. She seems to be at odds with her father, her brothers, and her family. . . .

Walker's father died in 1973, before she had effected a reconciliation with him, and his death aggravated her alienation before it propelled her toward confronting it. She told David Bradley: "'You know, his death was harder than I had thought at the time. We were so estranged that when I heard—I was in an airport somewhere—I didn't think I felt anything. It was years later that I really felt it. We had a wonderful reconciliation after he died.'" Walker's estrangement seems to date from her childhood accident. It also appears that her hardheartedness towards her father prevented her grieving for him until quite a while after his death. The year 1973 also marks Walker's last year in Mississippi, when she continued her struggles against depression and the urge to commit suicide: "My salvation that last year was a black woman psychiatrist who had also grown up in the South. Though she encouraged me to talk about whether or not I had loved and/or understood my father, I became increasingly aware that I was holding myself responsible for the conditions of black people in America. Unable to murder the oppressors, I sat in a book-lined study and wrote about lives. . . ." The correspondence between the issue that Walker holds against herself and that which precipitated her alienation from her father is startling: She feels just as inadequate at rescuing black people as she felt he was inadequate at rescuing her after the childhood accident.

As the concerns of her therapist suggest, Walker seems ignorant of her father's life. It may be this ignorance that she tried to relieve on the visit to her father's grave that she reports in the Bradley interview: "'I didn't cry when he died, but that summer I was in terrible shape. And I went to Georgia and I went to the cemetery and I laid down on top of his grave. I wanted to see what he could see, if he could look up. And I started to cry. And all the knottedness that had been in our relationship dissolved. And we're fine now.'" Since Walker elsewhere says that it took years for her to allow herself to grieve for her father, it is difficult to take literally this assertion of dissolved knottedness. Moreover, this account seems to undercut her 1975 statement concerning her father's sexism: "It was not until I became a student of women's liberation ideology that I could understand and forgive my father." The persona of the poem "Good Night, Willie Lee, I'll See You in the Morning" insists that there is real forgiveness of the father and a "healing / of all our wounds," but the more the persona speaks of forgiveness the less assured the reader feels that Walker's fundamental attitude towards her father has changed, especially when one considers her fictive portrayal of men. Yet it is certain that finding ways to forgive her father has been a continuing concern of Alice Walker's.

Folk Art as a Means to Female Survival

Keith E. Byerman

Keith E. Byerman, professor of English at Indiana State University in Terre Haute, is a prolific scholar in the field of African American studies, having written books and articles on such figures as Toni Morrison and W.E.B. DuBois.

In the following essay, Byerman notes that, ironically, The Color Purple *has many elements of the fairy tale or folktale. Celie is controlled by an evil stepparent as in "Cinderella," claims Byerman, and she is awakened from sleep by a kiss, as in "Sleeping Beauty." The fairy tale usually ends with the happy uniting of characters, as it does in* The Color Purple. *The means of resolution for women in the novel is, as it frequently is in folktales, the arts of singing, sewing, and quilting. In quilt making, asserts Byerman, torn pieces of cloth can be made whole, and a damaged woman can be healed. The other healing folk art Byerman identifies is the blues that lifts up Shug and, later, Squeak. Harpo turns his house into a home for the blues. Celie's pants-making business, Byerman writes, has connections to both folk art and fairy tales, but the happy ending necessarily takes place outside of the folk world.*

Writers Toni Cade Bambara and Alice Walker . . . tell stories of the initiations of black girls into womanhood, defining in the process the complex meaning of being black and female in a culture that has denigrated both qualities. As in the case of the male authors, they differ from each other, Bambara being primarily a short-story writer concentrating

Keith E. Byerman, "Chapter Three: Women's Blues: The Fiction of Toni Cade Bambara and Alice Walker," in *Fingering the Jagged Grain: Tradition and Form in Recent Black Fiction*. The University of Georgia Press, 1985. Copyright © 1985 University of Georgia Press. All rights reserved. Reproduced by permission.

on the northern urban experience while Walker, best known for her novels, emphasizes the rural and southern aspects of black life. . . . [T]hey are essentially traditional in their use of fictional forms, choosing as they do to represent the world in realistic terms. Those terms are frequently harsh and unconventional, but they remain within mimetic boundaries. Through such realism they present the experiences of black women, who are shown to suffer in the world but who also discover ways to endure and prosper, the latter usually in spiritual or psychological rather than material ways. The principal source of strength is the knowledge, gained through folk wisdom, that suffering seems the destiny of women and that survival is a valid revenge for the pain. Moreover, "living to tell about it" becomes a means of control, since the remembering refutes any claim that suffering and exploitation can be justified. The realistic structures of their fiction lend verisimilitude to the tales of racial and sexual oppression and triumph.

Overcoming the Oppressor

The thematic emphasis here is intentional; both writers tend toward feminist ideology, either in depicting the mistreatment of women or in asserting a superior female sensibility, gained largely through painful experience. Frequently, Walker and Bambara integrate this ideological position with folk values so that each enhances the other. Political concepts give direction and force to an often fatalistic folk wisdom; the realities of the folk link ideology to a concrete history. But this conjunction does not always work, since the folk worldview implicitly assumes that endurance rather than political power is its objective. It insists not on overcoming the enemy so much as outwitting and outliving him. These authors, in their more polemical moments, seek the means of supplanting the oppressor. The very language and structure of their folk sources, however, render their work more ambiguous than they seem to intend. Their occasionally ahistorical politics come into dialectical conflict with their historically conditioned cultural materials. Such a conflict makes for uneasy fictional structures where apparent resolution hides the absence of the very thing claimed. Despite themselves then, these fictions remain open rather than closed. . . .

The Color Purple (1982), Walker's award-winning and much-praised novel, has achieved immense popularity. In part, this success can be explained because the book is, in essence, a "womanist" fairy tale. Like Snow White, Celie is poisoned (psychologically in the novel) by an evil step-parent; like Cinderella, she is the ugly, abused daughter who ultimately becomes the princess; like Sleeping Beauty, she is awakened from her death-in-life by the kiss of a beloved; and like them all, she and her companions, after great travails, live happily ever after. Moreover, the fairy-tale quality is more than metaphoric, since major plot elements are worked out with fairy-tale devices. . . . Celie is told by her evil stepfather, after he rapes her, that she must tell no one but God what he has done; she chooses to write her story, which, as shall be seen below, makes it a public text. Transformation from a life of shame to one of self-esteem occurs when Celie receives the physical embrace of the regal Shug Avery. Finally, the plot is resolved and the characters reunited through the exposure of villainy and the death of the primary villain, an event which reverses the dispossession of Celie and her sister Nettie.

African American Folk Culture

Since the fairy tale itself is a folk form, albeit a European one, there is no obvious contradiction between it and the Afro-American and African materials that enrich the narrative. In fact, such materials enhance the sense of a faerie world where curses, coincidences, and transformations are possible. The power for healing and change latent in folk arts and practices important to black women—quilting, mothering, blues singing, "craziness," and conjure—fit the pattern of the female character in the fairy tale who is victimized but then saved through love and magic. One of the things that mark Walker's text as womanist is her insistence that these female capacities are a superior way of bringing about change. One trait that distinguishes *The Color Purple* from her earlier work is her setting up of an opposition between male and female folk wisdom; the former wisdom, passed from father to son, claims, in Walker's view, the natural inferiority of women and the need to keep them under control, through violence if necessary. . . .

The dominating male voice is present as the first words of the narrative: "You better not never tell nobody but God. It'd kill your mammy." These statements simultaneously demand female silence and place the responsibility for illicit behavior on the woman. They are spoken by the man Celie believes to be her father after he has raped her. In effect, he makes her voice rather than his action the fatal force in the family. By his definition, it is not his violation of taboo but Celie's violation of his command that will kill the mother. He presumes that his rules of order transcend those of the social order. But silence does not protect the women; the mother dies anyway, and Celie continues to be sexually assaulted. In fact, the father uses the silence as evidence of acquiescence to his desires. Neither Celie nor her mother exists for him except as ciphers to which he can arbitrarily assign meanings.

Appropriately, in this context, Celie chooses to write rather than speak to God. At one point, Nettie recalls a comment by her sister: "I remember one time you said your life made you feel so ashamed you couldn't even talk about it to God, you had to write it, bad as you thought your writing was." On the one hand, the statement suggests the effectiveness of the father's threat; one so degraded as Celie denies herself even the most private speech act. Nonetheless, she can write. In this sense, the process of writing is itself associated with shame; it is the expression of those beyond salvation, those who have been dehumanized. Writing, then, takes on those characteristics of the disreputable that, as indicated earlier, are linked with the folk culture. In entering the culture, it becomes dialectical. For example, the act of writing, though apparently motivated by Celie's desire to obey the original interdiction against speech, is clearly a violation of the command. Spoken words are transient; writing lasts as long as ink and paper. By putting down her thoughts, Celie makes possible discovery of her pain and victimization. The fundamental violation here is that she writes herself into humanity and thereby contradicts the stipulation that she be a mere cipher. She gives herself an inner life and a concrete history and thus an otherness that the patriarchal order denies her. In the folk tradition, then, her letters subvert oppression in the process of affirming it. . . .

Female Support from Quilting

The role of the blues singer, to be discussed in more detail below, is only one of the folk images in the book. Quilting, for example, functions as a way of creating female community in a world that represses female expression. Early in the story, Celie, who has largely accepted the male definition of woman's place, advises Harpo to beat his new wife into submission. She does this in part because she has trouble with the concept of an independent woman, since such a figure implicitly calls into question her own submissiveness. When Sofia confronts her with the consequences of her advice, she cannot adequately explain her action, but faces for the first time her hatred of her own womanhood. This awareness enables the two of them to establish rapport through the folk arts of the dozens and quilt-making. The exchange of insults allows them to vent any remaining hostility:

> I'm *so* shame of myself, I say. And the Lord he done whip me little bit too.
>
> The Lord don't like ugly, she say.

And he ain't stuck on pretty.

This open the way for our talk to turn another way.

This ritual, usually associated with males, creates an equality and intimacy between them that guilt and anger had previously made impossible. It leads to the quilting, which has a healing influence: "Let's make quilt pieces out of these messed up curtains, she say. And I run git my pattern book. I sleeps like a baby now." Later on, sewing on the quilt occasions opportunities to discuss various problems; moreover, the process itself is a way of literally keeping one's history. The yellow stars Celie makes out of Shug's dress recall the designs she used to make for her daughter Olivia's diapers. And in Africa, Nettie uses a quilt to force that daughter's adoptive mother to remember Celie, a recollection that absolves Nettie of accusations against her and that allows Corrine to die in peace....

Refusing to Accept the Rules

Afro-American women ... develop with models for resistance as well as healing. The first of these is the "crazy" woman.... The story of Sofia is explicitly the story of a woman who will not accept the rules of an oppressive order. She refuses to allow Harpo to beat her and in fact always wins their physical battles; some of the most humorous moments in the book are his attempts to explain away his inability to control her: "He say, Oh, me and that mule. She fractious, you know. She went crazy in the field the other day. By time I got her to head for home I was all banged up. Then when I got home, I walked smack dab into the crib door. Hit my eye and scratch my chin. Then when that storm come up last night I shet the window down on my hand." Her more serious struggles are against white authority figures who presume to dictate her role. She talks back to the mayor's wife and then strikes the mayor when he attempts physically to put her "in her place." She is then beaten by the police and thrown in jail for assault. In prison, she constantly dreams of murder....

Celie herself functions at one point as a conjure woman. When she decides to travel to Memphis with Shug, she delivers herself of a curse on Mr. _____: "Until you do right by me, I say, everything you even dream about will fail. I give it to him straight, just like it come to me. And it seem to come to me from the trees." Walker uses here [Harlem Renaissance writer] Zora Neale Hurston's notion that the voice speaking is in fact that of a god using a human instrument: "A dust devil flew up on the porch between us, fill my mouth with dirt. The dirt say, Anything you do to me, already done to you." The voice, whatever its source, speaks the truth of Celie's pent-up anger and sense of injustice. Speaking forth carries with it its own authority; the voice exposes the suffering that has been her life and gives her an interiority and humanity that others have denied her. Her conjuring, in other words, has creative moral force. Its effect is shown in Mr. _____'s decline, both physical and mental, during her absence; only when he takes steps to right the wrongs he has done her does his strength return. Significantly, his major wrong has been the withholding of correspondence between Celie and Nettie. When he accepts their right to expression, the curse is lifted.

Shug as Survivor and Inspiration

The most important of the folk figures is the female blues singer Shug Avery.

Her most complex effect is on Celie. From the very beginning she makes a powerful impression: "Shug Avery was a woman. The most beautiful woman I ever saw. She more pretty than my mama. She bout ten thousand times more prettier then me. I see her there in furs. Her face rouge. Her hair like somethin tail. She grinning with her foot up on somebody motocar. Her eyes serious tho. Sad some." Shug exists as something other than the reality in which Celie lives, and yet she is connected with that reality through Mr. _____. Thus she is not pure fantasy, a being representing escape from the harsh world of the present. The seriousness and sadness in her face suggest that she too has had unpleasant experiences and has lived through them. In addition, she opens for Celie the realm of the unconscious, giving this cipher another dimension of being. . . .

Shug as a folk figure opens possibilities rather than constructs completed orders of reality.

However, another of her contributions to creativity leads to a resolution of the text's conflicts that is more appropriate to the fairy tale than to Afro-American folklore. At her suggestion, Celie begins making pants, especially purple ones (a color associated with Shug's regal bearing), for herself and others. At first, this traditional art works in a folk manner; though she desires to kill Albert for suppressing the letters, she puts her energy into sewing instead: "A needle and not a razor in my hand, I think." But, when the immediate motive passes, pants making becomes a business and Celie a petty capitalist who turns her farm into a home factory. When it is revealed that Albert has always enjoyed sewing, any lingering hostility vanishes, and they sit on the porch stitching "folksy" pants and shirts.

Final Union in a Feminine Community

This resolution is part of a larger pattern of closure in the narrative. Harpo turns his house into a blues club where Shug and Mary Agnes sing, while he works at his favorite activity, cooking. When the stepfather dies, a long-hidden will appears which shows that the land, house, and store he had possessed for years in fact were left to Celie and Nettle. And, finally, the long-lost sister escapes from Africa and turns up at the farm with Celie's children, Olivia and Adam, who has scarified his own face to identify himself with the suffering womanhood of his African bride. Thus, all the characters are reunited in a feminized space with female traits and free of the hostility, oppression, guilt and cruelty of the male and white worlds.

But this very liberation contradicts the nature of the folk sensibility on which it is based. History, with the suffering and joy it brings, cannot, in the folk worldview, be transcended; it must be lived through. Walker seeks to resolve the dialectic by making all males female (or at least androgynous), all destroyers creators, and all difference sameness. In this process, she must move outside the very conflicts that generated the sewing, the blues singing, and the voice of Celie herself. Such an effort makes sense for one who wishes to articulate a political position; resolution creates a sacred, utopian space which justifies the ideology on which it is based. But this creation is in fact another system that requires the same denial of history and difference as the order it has supplanted. To live "happily ever after," as the folk characters do in *The Color Purple*, is, ironically, to live outside the folk world.

Male Cruelty Leads to Positive Changes

Henry O. Dixon

Henry O. Dixon, who received his doctorate from Clark Atlanta University, is a professor at Morehouse College and the author of Male Protagonists.

In a somewhat unusual approach, in this article Dixon examines the way in which the cruelty of black men in Celie's life gives her greater impetus to achieve her selfhood and independence than she would have otherwise had. At least in the case of Albert, the consequences of his abuse bring on a positive change in his character, argues Dixon. Her stepfather turns to an abusive control of his family to assuage an ego bruised by white culture. When he cannot control his wife, who refuses him, he turns on Celie. According to Dixon, the stepfather's abuse of Celie gives her the power to protect her sister from him, and later, from Mister. Celie's marriage to Albert is an unspeakably brutal one. Yet, Dixon argues, it changes Celie and Albert for the better after they have gone their separate ways. Furthermore, Celie gets to know and be taught by Sofia and Shug. Albert's concealment of Celie's sister's letters is the final straw, the episode that gives her the strength to leave Albert, move to Memphis, and become independent, according to Dixon. This jolts Albert out of his insensitive bullying and makes a new and better man of him, Dixon concludes.

Although [Alice] Walker places the African-American woman at the focal point of the fiction [in *The Color Purple*], the male characters play crucial and significant roles

Henry O. Dixon, "Chapter Three: Oppression and Development: Men in *The Color Purple*," in *Male Protagonists in Four Novels of Alice Walker: Destruction and Development in Interpersonal Relationships.* The Edwin Mellen Press, 2007. Copyright © 2007 The Edwin Mellen Press. All rights reserved. Reproduced by permission.

in the development of Celie's character and in her final transformation. Mister or Albert, the only names that Walker gives him in the novel, is the most important male character in Celie's development. However, Celie writes about other male characters who affect her character. Through their brutal behavior, the men ironically contribute to Celie's growth and development, permitting her to define her own womanhood. Therefore, . . . the men, inevitably, play decisive and important roles in Celie's growth and development. [This article] will explore, also, the hypothesis that although men abuse Celie in an effort to dominate and victimize her, their abuse actually enables Celie to assert herself, overcome their oppression, and move toward contentment and independence. . . .

Using Cruelty to Maintain Control

In Celie's first life in *The Color Purple*, the first male character whom the reader learns about is Fonso. Fonso lives in rural Georgia in the 1900s. When he appears in the novel, he is a married adult with stepchildren. He is a poor, Southern African-American man who is virtually uneducated and . . . like Walker's other male characters in her earlier novels, lives in a white American social structure that dictates his entire attitude. These limitations, once imposed on his life, do not allow Fonso to know his full potential, to know himself, or even to know, evaluate, or develop important values in his life. The distorted values cause Fonso to develop a poor self-concept and an extremely low self-esteem. He is powerless and possibly humiliated by his condition in life. He feels limited and restricted. In reprisal for his own oppressive condition, Fonso feels the need to be dominant and aggressive in his family, which leads him to physically, sexually, and psychologically abuse the women with whom he comes in contact in the novel. Fonso, however, . . . never changes or reforms his abusive behavior toward women in the novel, and he eventually destroys himself by his own selfish acts of sexual indulgence.

The first evidence of Fonso's abuse of women begins with Celie's mother. Fonso attempts to force Celie's mother to engage in sexual intercourse with him shortly after she has had a baby son, Lucious, and at a time when she is seriously ill. However, Fonso is rejected by Celie's mother, and such rejection and restriction by his own wife render him impotent in his control of the situation at home. He feels even more powerless and frustrated, and his manhood—defined primarily through sex—is seriously threatened and violated:

> Last spring after little Lucious come I heard them fussing. He was pulling on her arm. She say it too soon, Fonso, I ain't well. Finally he leave her alone. A week go by, he pulling on her arm again. She say Naw, I ain't gonna. Can't you see I'm already half dead, and all of these children.

Celie's mother's refusal to engage in sexual intercourse with Fonso leads Fonso to begin to feel the need to reestablish his control and male domination within the family. To ensure that his control is never violated again, in any way, he realizes that he must intensify his control of women in his life. Therefore, to further demonstrate his disapproval of Celie's mother's rejection and restriction and the resulting threats and violations of his manhood, Fonso rapes Celie, his stepdaughter, to fulfill his sexual desires and to reestablish his male domination in the family: "[Celie's mother] went to visit her sister doctor over Macon. Left me to see after the others. He never had a kine word to say to me. Just say 'You gonna do what your mammy wouldn't.'"

Celie's Developing Identity

As a result of reestablishing his male domination in the family, Celie, the protagonist in the novel, becomes the second female whom Fonso abuses. When the action begins, Celie is portrayed as a lonely, isolated, and abused fourteen-year-old girl who lives in southern rural Georgia. At that early age . . . Celie is not in control of her own life or of her own body; her

In the novel The Color Purple, *Celie (played by Whoopi Goldberg in the film version) eventually finds the strength to leave her abusive husband, Albert (Danny Glover).* © Photo 12/Alamy.

stepfather, Fonso, is in control, and physical, sexual, and psychological abuse overpowers Celie from the age of fourteen to early adulthood. He forces and frightens her into sexual submission, the consequences of which are two pregnancies; Fonso further abuses Celie by immediately taking her babies from her. He restricts her by forbidding her to tell anyone of the brutal rapes that he inflicts on her young body, and he dishonors her when he becomes attracted to her younger sister Nettie. Celie is no longer sexually attractive to him; she is not a virgin; she is worthless to him. He tells Mister: "She the oldest anyway. She ought to marry first. She ain't fresh tho. . . . She spoiled. Twice. . . . And she a bad influence on my other girls." Fonso shows his continued lack of character by finding and marrying a girl Celie's age. His new wife, now that Celie's mother is dead, can do what Celie cannot do—bear children.

Fonso's abuse, intended to control and restrict Celie, paradoxically begins to contribute to Celie's initial stage of development. Celie begins to fight back and to begin her journey toward identity, development, and independence. First, Fonso's abuse causes Celie to develop an alternative relationship with God. In God she finds a refuge. He is not abusive. He is understanding, loving, and caring. Therefore, she begins to write letters to God because He is the only One to whom she can turn to tell her troubles. . . .

When "Mister" Does Not Get His Way

During Celie's second life, Mister is the next male character whom the reader meets. Walker does not provide the reader with information about his childhood other than a description of an early sewing experience with his mother. As [Mister] grows into adulthood, the reader learns that there are times when he is happy. He loves to dance and to laugh. . . . Mister tells Celie later in the novel about his first wife and how he and Shug "messed over" her. These problems came as a result of Mister's father's refusal to allow him to marry the woman of his choice. He was also denied the woman of his choice by Fonso, who refuses to allow him to marry Nettie. Instead, he is forced to marry Celie, whom he treats brutally until she rebels and leaves him.

Because Mister is denied the woman of his choice, he takes on the values he inherits from his father. He becomes a womanizer and a child-abuser. Mister beats women because it makes him feel dominant and aggressive, in control of the situation and the decisions that are made; he no longer feels victimized and powerless.

Consequently, Celie becomes his servant, and Mister exercises full control over her. He controls her by dictating her life and forcing her to obey his commands. Celie is forced to work in the fields and in the house and to take care of Mister's unruly and intractable children. Mister invariably beats her and reduces her womanly status even in the presence of his own children. . . .

A Violent Marriage Opens a New World

Although Celie is in a withdrawn and restrained emotional state, Mister's marriage to her provides her an opportunity to develop several close relationships with a male character in the novel: Harpo, Mister's oldest son. Initially, Harpo dislikes Celie because he refuses to accept her as his mother. However, as the plot develops Harpo begins to confide in Celie. As his counselor, Celie offers him what little wisdom she has garnered from her years of abuse by the men in her own downtrodden life. Celie writes: "I think bout this when Harpo ast me what he ought to do to her [his wife] to make her mind. . . . Beat her, I say." Harpo's conversation with Celie provides Celie with a catharsis that allows her to begin to release and eliminate her own tensions and emotions. As a result, Celie discovers that she can not only write her feelings and aspirations, but she can also express them orally. Besides, Harpo's relationship with Celie permits her to visit his juke-joint and to come in contact with other people in the community.

Equally importantly, Mister's marriage to Celie brings her in contact with Sofia, Harpo's wife, with whom Celie develops a close relationship. When Celie mistakenly advises Harpo to beat Sofia, Sofia angrily confronts Celie for giving him such advice. As a result of this confrontation, the women are able to resolve their differences, and a close relationship ensues. . . . When Celie tells Sofia how cruel and brutal Mister is to her, Sofia seriously advises Celie: "You ought to bash Mister's head open. . . . Think bout heaven later."

Although Mister's control and abuse force Celie to retreat into an unfortunate emotional state, it is his rejection of her that eventually contributes to her growth. Mister rejects Celie by bringing Shug Avery, his mistress, into their home. Although Mister's inviting of Shug into their home is intended to further abuse Celie by replacing her in her own home, his action actually produces an opposite effect. That is, instead of forcing Celie and Shug to become bitter adversaries, the situation allows them to become intimate friends. Much of this intimacy, on Celie's part, comes as a result of the abuse inflicted on her by men, forcing her to reject heterosexual relationships. It is this rejection of heterosexual relationships that leads Celie to accept an alternative relationship, free of violence and abuse, with Shug. Thus, Mister's rejection of Celie, like Fonso's denunciation and rejection of her, contributes to Celie's growth and development. . . .

Celie Frees Herself

As Celie reflects on how Mister has concealed so much information from her, her resentment and hatred of Mister increase and, as a result of his concealing Nettie's letters and of the many years of abuse inflicted on her, she rebels and confronts several situations in her life. She confronts Fonso and tells him that he is not her biological father: "I feels so sick I almost gag. Nettie in Africa, I say. A missionary. She wrote me that you ain't our real Pa." She crushes Mister's ego by avenging herself for Mister's cruel behavior. She openly degrades and embarrasses him: "You a lowdown dog is what's wrong, I say. It's time to leave you and enter into the Creation. And your dead body just the welcome mat I need." She renounces and rejects God because she feels that He has rejected her, as have the other men in her life: "I don't write to God no more. . . . I say, the God I been praying and writing to is a man. And act just like all the other mens I know. Trifling, forgetful and lowdown". . .

Mister's abuse, intended to restrict and control Celie, pushes her to a third life where she moves toward identity and independence through her own productivity and creativity. . . .

The Change in Mister

While Celie is developing her own creativity in the art of sewing, reforming her life, and feeling free of male brutality in Memphis, Mister is gradually reforming himself in rural Georgia. Ironically, in this process it is Celie's independence from male brutality that leads Mister to transform himself. Mister begins his transformation by reflecting and questioning his past life of neglect and abuse of his first wife, Annie Julia, Celie, his second wife, and his children. Mister realizes that he has allowed the joy in his life to pass him by, and he feels only regretful misery regarding his abuse of them and the life he has lived. In fact, as he questions the need to love, to suffer, and to be African-American men and women, and as he questions his knowledge of his own environment, it does not take him long to realize that he has learned nothing:

> Anyhow, he say, you know how it is. You ast yourself one question, it lead to fifteen. I start to wonder why us need love. Why us suffer. Why us black. Why men and women. Where do children come from. It didn't take me long to realize I didn't hardly know nothing. And that if you ast yourself why you black or a man or a woman or a bush it don't mean nothing if you don't ast why you here, period.

In addition, Mister tells Celie about his theorem of reflection and how it leads to love:

> I think us here to wonder, myself. To wonder, To ast. And that in wondering bout the big things and asting bout the big things, you learn about the little ones, almost by accident. But you never know nothing more about the big things than you start out with. The more I wonder . . . the more I love.

It is during this period of pondering and reflecting on his past life that Mister becomes enlightened. This enlightenment helps him to discover himself and, eventually, to love himself and others around him. . . .

Parallel Transformations

As a result of Mister's counseling and his demonstration of concern for Celie, both Mister and Celie reach a supreme plane of spirituality through love and forgiveness. Celie, who has learned to love and to forgive, forgives Mister for his past record of abuse of her and realizes that he has redefined his manhood and reformed himself. Celie writes to Nettie:

> After all the evil he done I know you wonder why I don't hate him. I don't hate him for two reasons. One, he love Shug. And two, Shug use to love him. Plus, look like he trying to make something out of himself. I don't mean just that he work and he clean up after himself and he appreciate some of the things God was playful enough to make. I mean when you talk to him now he really listen, and one time, out of nowhere in the conversation us was having, he said Celie, I'm satisfied this the first time I ever lived on Earth as a natural man. It feel like a natural experience.

As a result of Mister's transformation, Celie is enabled to make her final transformation. Celie now knows that she is free of the burden of Mister's abuse and of all men. She feels contented and independent:

> Then the old devil put his arms around me and just stood there on the porch with me real quiet. Way after while I bent my stiff neck onto his shoulder. Here us is, I thought, two old fools left over from love, keeping each other company under the stars.

Celie's transformation at this juncture in the novel helps her confidently to define and accept her own sexuality and womanhood. She is sure that she and Mister—Albert, the name she finally calls him—can be friends only, even though he has asked her to marry him again, "this time in the spirit as well as in the flesh." Celie, however, refuses him. Moreover, Celie resolves the conflict in her mind about Shug: "If she come, I be happy. If she don't, I be content. And then I figure this the lesson I was suppose to learn." As a result, Mister and Celie develop a closer, friendlier, and more fulfilling relationship. Celie, like Mister, accepts her new life of contentment and independence, as she eagerly waits to be reunited with her sister and her children at the end of the novel. . . .

In *The Color Purple*, Walker demonstrates that a man's violent, abusive, and sadistic behavior, intended to control and restrict a woman, can often actually contribute to a woman's growth and development. First, a man's behavior may cause a woman to search for alternative relationships, because there are alternatives for women who are constantly abused and rejected. Secondly, the novel demonstrates that a man's abuse may force a woman to revolt and to join forces with other women, and it is this revolt and networking that can bring a man to himself. Thirdly, a man's abuse may cause a woman to leave or escape to a more productive and creative environment in which she can redefine her identity and accept her "rite of passage" into a world of independence and freedom. Finally, the novel demonstrates that when a woman leaves a man, he frequently can begin to reflect and to reevaluated his life and eventually to have a conversion that enables him to transcend his violent, abusive, and sadistic behavior and to contribute to a wholesome and productive relationship with a woman. Thus, the novel ends with such a conversion and a transcendence when Mister contributes to humanly profitable relationships with Celie and others in the novel.

Centering on Women but Ignoring Race and Economics

bell hooks

A prominent figure as an activist and author, bell hooks (the pen name of Gloria Watkins) has held academic positions at Yale, Oberlin, and City College of New York, among others, and is currently Distinguished Professor in Residence at Berea College in her home state of Kentucky. She is the author of a number of books, including Ain't I a Woman? *and* Communion.

In this essay, bell hooks reminds the reader that spiritualism and materialism are usually regarded as philosophical opposites. After all, materialism demanded a system of slavery and later misuse of African American labor. But in hooks's view, Alice Walker unites spiritualism and materialism in The Color Purple. *Although Celie is exploited by a patriarchal materialism that cannot prevail without using people like Celie, her own mastery of capitalism as a manager, producer, and independent businesswoman is presented as positive and liberating. Her materialism is benevolent, and she is not regarded as a threat. Sofia is her opposite in insisting on a self-assertion that constantly causes her to be injured. So, in a sense, Celie joins the system while Sofia fights it. Hooks contends that the difference between the ways in which white and African American rape is regarded in the novel borders on racism. The evils of exploitation are attributed almost solely to sexism while racism is ignored, and the novel fails to challenge the economic system behind these evils, hooks concludes.*

Presuming a female spectator (women and specifically white women from privileged classes are the primary audience for women-centered novels), [Alice Walker] constructs a fiction in which it is the masculine threat, represented by black masculinity, that must be contained, controlled, and ultimately transformed. Her most radical re-visioning of the oppressive patriarchal social order is her insistence on the transformation of Mr. ———. He moves from male oppressor to enlightened being, willingly surrendering his attachment to the phallocentric social order reinforced by the sexual oppression of women. His transformation begins when Celie threatens his existence, when her curse disempowers him. Since sexuality and power are so closely linked to politics of domination, Mr. ——— must be completely desexualized as part of the transformative process. . . .

Contradiction and Confusion

Spiritual quest is connected with the effort of characters in *The Color Purple* to be more fully self-realized. This effort merges in an unproblematic way with a materialist ethic which links acquisition of goods with the capacity to experience emotional well-being. Traditionally mystical experience is informed by radical critique and renunciation of materialism. Walker positively links the two. Even though her pronounced critique of patriarchy includes an implicit indictment of perverse individualism which encourages exploitation (Albert is transformed in part by his rejection of isolation and self-sufficiency for connection and interdependency), Celie's shift from underclass victim to capitalist entrepreneur has only positive signification. Albert, in his role as oppressor, forces Celie and Harpo to work in the fields, exploiting their labor for his gain. Their exploitation as workers must cease before domination ends and transformation begins. Yet Celie's progression from exploited black woman, as woman, as sexual victim, is aided by her entrance into the economy as property owner, manager of a small business, storekeeper—in short, capitalist entrepreneur. No attention is accorded aspects of this enterprise that might reinforce domination: attention is focused on how useful Celie's pants are for family and friends; on the way Sofia as worker in her store will treat black customers with respect and consideration. Embedded in the construction of sexual difference as it is characterized in *The Color Purple* is the implicit assumption that women are innately less inclined to oppress and dominate than men; that women are not easily corrupted.

Rewarded with economic prosperity for her patient endurance of suffering, Celie never fully develops capacities for sustained self-assertion. Placed on a moral pedestal which allows no one to see her as a threat, she is always a potential victim. By contrast, Sofia's self-affirmation, her refusal to see herself as victim, is not rewarded. She is consistently punished. Sadly, as readers witness Celie's triumph, her successful effort to resist male domination which takes place solely in a private familial context, we also bear witness to Sofia's tragic fate, as she resists sexist and racist oppression in private and public spheres. Unlike Celie or Shug, she is regarded as a serious threat to the social order and is violently attacked, brutalized, and subdued. Always a revolutionary, Sofia has never been victimized or complicit in her own oppression. . . .

A Happy Ending Based in Fantasy

The values expressed in woman bonding—mutuality, respect, shared power, and unconditional love—become guiding principles shaping the new community in *The Color Purple* which includes everyone, women and men, family and kin. Reconstructed black males, Harpo and Albert are active participants expanding the circle of care. Together this extended kin network affirms the primacy of a revitalized spirituality in which everything that exists is informed by godliness, in which love as a force that affirms connection and intersubjective communion makes an erotic metaphysic possible. Forgiveness and compassion enable individuals who were estranged and alienated to nurture one another's growth. The message conveyed in the novel that relationships no matter how seriously impaired can be restored is compelling. Distinct from the promise of a happy ending, it allows for the recognition of conflict and pain, for the possibility of reconciliation. . . .

When the novel concludes, Celie has everything her oppressor has wanted and more—relationships with chosen loved ones; land ownership; material wealth; control over the labor of others. She is happy. In a *Newsweek* interview, Walker makes the revealing statement, "I liberated Celie from her own history. I wanted her to be happy." Happiness is not subject to re-vision, radicalization. The terms are familiar, absence of conflict, pain, and struggle; a fantasy of every desire fulfilled. Given these terms, Walker creates a fiction wherein an oppressed black woman can experience self-recovery without a dialectical process; without collective political effort; without radical change in society.

Oppressive Structures Remain

To make Celie happy she creates a fiction where struggle—the arduous and painful process by which the oppressed work for liberation—has no place. This fantasy of change without effort is a dangerous one for both oppressed and oppressor. It is a brand of false consciousness that keeps everyone in place and oppressive structures intact. It is just this distortion of reality that Walker warns against in her essay "If the Present Looks Like the Past":

> In any case, the duty of the writer is not to be tricked, seduced, or goaded into verifying by imitation or even rebuttal other people's fantasies. In an oppressive society it may well be that all fantasies indulged in by the oppressor are destructive to the oppressed. To become involved in them in any way at all is, at the very least, to lose time defining yourself.

For oppressed and oppressor the process of liberation—individual self-realization and revolutionary transformation of society—requires confrontation with reality, the letting go of fantasy. Speaking of his loathing for fantasy [acclaimed author] Gabriel García Márquez explains:

> I believe the imagination is just an instrument for producing reality and that the source of creation is always, in the last instance, reality. Fantasy, in the sense of pure and simple Walt Disney-style invention without any basis in reality is the most loathsome thing of all. . . . Children don't like fantasy either. What they do like is imagination. The difference between the one and the other is the same as between a human being and a ventriloquist's dummy.

The tragedy embedded in the various happy endings in *The Color Purple* can be located at that point where fantasy triumphs over imagination, where creative power is suppressed. While this diminishes the overall aesthetic power of *The Color Purple*, it does not render meaningless those crucial moments in the text where the imagination works to liberate, to challenge, to make the new—real and possible. These moments affirm the integrity of artistic vision, restore and renew.

The Color Purple Is a Disservice to Black Women

Trudier Harris

A prominent scholar of African American culture, Trudier Harris is the J. Carlyle Sitterson Professor Emerita at the University of North Carolina at Chapel Hill. She is also the author and editor of some twenty books, including The Scary Mason-Dixon Line *(2009).*

In this selection, Harris departs from the laudatory praise of Alice Walker's depiction of black women in The Color Purple *to plead for a more incisive, independent examination of the novel's flaws. From the first, she disagrees with the canonization of the novel. The fact that it is a well-written novel by an African American woman about the suffering of an African American woman, garnering high praise from white critics, has tended to silence comments from black female critics. Harris, on the other hand, is vocal in her objections to Walker's portraits of women in the novel, especially Celie, who is subservient and accepts, largely without complaint or resistance, the abuse inflicted on her. Harris takes issue with feminist Gloria Steinem's praise of the novel's morality, citing details of the novel's moral failure. Harris also points out the novel's stereotyping of both black men and women, including the unrealistic weakness of Celie and the view of males as mindless sadists. She finds the novel's ending to be more of a fairy tale than a realistic portrait.*

*T*he Color Purple has been canonized. I don't think it should have been. The tale of the novel's popularity is the tale of the media's ability, once again, to dictate the tastes of the reading public, and to attempt to shape what is acceptable

Trudier Harris, "On *The Color Purple*, Stereotypes, and Silence," *Black American Literature Forum*, vol. 18, Winter 1984. Copyright © 1984 by Black American Literature Forum. Reproduced by permission.

creation by black American writers. Sadly, a book that might have been ignored if it had been published ten years earlier or later has now become *the* classic novel by a black woman. . . .

Popularity Tends to Silence Criticism

The Color Purple silences by its dominance, a dominance perpetuated by the popular media. Those who initially found or still find themselves unable to speak out perhaps reflect in some way my own path to writing about the novel. From the time the novel appeared in 1982, I have been waging a battle with myself to record my reaction to it. For me, the process of reading, re-reading, and re-reading the novel, discussing it, then writing about it has reflected some of the major dilemmas of the black woman critic. To complain about the novel is to commit treason against black women writers, yet there is much in it that deserves complaint, and there are many black women critics in this country who would rather have their wisdom teeth pulled than be accused of objecting to it. After all, a large number of readers, usually vocal and white, have decided that *The Color Purple* is the quintessential statement on Afro-American women and a certain kind of black lifestyle in these United States.

My dilemma started in Alabama in July of 1982 when I completed the novel and went into a fit of cursing for several days. Here, I felt, was a novel that had done a great disservice through its treatment of black women and a disservice as well to the Southern black communities in which such treatment was set. I couldn't imagine a Celie existing in any black community I knew or any that I could conceive of. What sane black woman, I asked, would sit around and take that crock of shit from all those folks? How long would it take her before she reached the stage of stabbing somebody to death, blowing somebody's head off, or at least going upside somebody's head? But the woman just sat there, like a bale of cotton with a vagina, taking stuff from kids even and waiting for someone to come along and rescue her. I had problems with that. And so did other black women. By contrast, most of the white women with whom I talked loved the novel.

Praise by White Women

When I started asking black women how they felt about the book, there was a quiet strain of discomfort with it, a quiet tendency to criticize, but none of them would do so very aggressively. We were all faced with the idea that to criticize a novel that had been so universally complimented was somehow a desertion of the race and the black woman writer. Yet, there was a feeling of uneasiness with the novel. Instead of focusing upon the specifics of that uneasiness, however, most of the black women with whom I talked preferred instead to praise that which they thought was safe: the beautiful voice in the book and Walker's ability to capture an authentic black folk speech without all the caricature that usually typifies such efforts. They could be lukewarm toward the relationship between Celie and Shug and generally criticize Albert. However, they almost never said anything about the book's African sections until I brought them up. Do they work for you? Do you see how they're integrated into the rest of the novel? Does the voice of Nettie ring authentic and true to you? Only when assured that their ideas would not be looked upon as a desertion of black femininity would the women then proceed to offer valuable insights.

For others, though, silence about the novel was something not to be broken. One Afro-American woman critic who has written on contemporary black women writers told me that she would never write anything on the novel or make a public statement about it. Quite clearly, that was a statement in itself. Her avowed silence became a political confirmation of everything that I found problematic about the novel.

Whoopi Goldberg plays a subservient and submissive Celie in Steven Spielberg's film adaptation of The Color Purple. *The Picture Desk.*

But shouldn't black women allow for diversity of interpretation of our experiences, you may ask? And shouldn't we be reluctant to prescribe a direction for our black women writers? Of course, but what we have with this novel is a situation in which many black women object to the portrayals of the characters, yet we may never hear the reasons for their objections precisely *because they are black women.*

I met many vocally articulate white women in 1982 and 1983 who loved *The Color Purple* and who are still singing its praises. Because I do not automatically assume that white women have my best interests at heart, I kept wondering why they so favored the novel when I myself had so many questions about it. In [feminist] Gloria Steinem's article on Alice Walker and her works, especially *The Color Purple*, which appeared in *Ms. Magazine* in July of 1982, Steinem reflects her own surprise at Walker's achievement; her response is condescending at times to a degree even beyond that latitude that might be expected in such works. She praises Walker for generally being alive, black, and able to write well. . . .

The Novel's Moral Failure

[Celie's] voice led to Steinem's celebration of the wonderful morality in the novel, yet what she finds so attractive provides another source of my contention with the book. Steinem asserts that morality for Walker "is not an external dictate. It doesn't matter if you love the wrong people, or have children with more than one of them, or whether you have money, go to church, or obey the laws. What matters is cruelty, violence, keeping the truth from others who need it, suppressing someone's will or talent, taking more than you need from people or nature, and failing to choose for yourself. It's the internal morality of dignity, autonomy, and balance." What kind of morality is it that espouses that all human degradation is justified if the individual somehow survives all the tortures and uglinesses heaped upon her? Where is the dignity, autonomy, or balance in that? I am not opposed to triumph, but I do have objections to the unrealistic presentation of the path, the *process* that leads to such a triumph, especially when it is used to create a new archetype or to resurrect old myths about black women.

By no means am I suggesting that Celie should be blamed for what happens to her. My problem is with her reaction to the situation. Even slave women who found themselves abused frequently found ways of responding to that—by running away, fighting back, poisoning their masters, or through more subtly defiant acts such as spitting into the food they cooked for their masters. They did something, and Celie shares a kinship in conception if not in chronology with them. . . .

Racial Stereotypes

I found so many white women who joined Steinem in praising the novel that I read it again just to recheck my own evaluations. Then, since I was on leave at The Bunting Institute at Radcliffe [College] and had access to a community of women, the majority of whom were white, I thought it would be fitting to test some of my ideas on them. Accordingly, I wrote a thirty-three-page article on the novel and invited women in residence at the Institute to come to a working paper session and respond to what I had written. My basic contentions were that the portrayal of Celie was unrealistic for the time in which the novel was set, that Nettie and the letters from Africa were really extraneous to the central concerns of the novel, that the lesbian relationship in the book represents the height of silly romanticism, and that the epistolary form of the novel ultimately makes Celie a much more sophisticated character than we are initially led to believe.

Twelve women, ten of them white, read the novel and came to my discussion of it over lunch. Several of them also read my paper. During that session, I discovered that some white women did not like the novel, but they were not the ones controlling publications like *Ms.* One white woman commented that, if she had not been told the novel had been written by a black woman, she would have thought it had been written by a Southern white male who wanted to reinforce the traditional sexual and violent stereotypes about black people. That comment affirmed one of my major objections to the thematic development of the novel: The book simply added a freshness to many of the ideas circulating in the popular culture and captured in racist literature that suggested that black people have no morality when it comes to sexuality, that black family structure is weak if existent at all, that black men abuse black women, and that black women who may appear to be churchgoers are really lewd and lascivious.

The novel gives validity to all the white racist's notions of pathology in black communities. For these spectator readers, black fathers and father-figures are viewed as being immoral, sexually unrestrained. Black males and females form units without the benefit of marriage, or they easily dissolve marriages in order to form less structured, more promiscuous relationships. Black men beat their wives—or attempt to—and neglect, ignore, or abuse their children. When they cannot control their wives through beatings, they violently dispatch them. The only stereotype that is undercut in the book is that of the matriarch. Sofia . . . is beaten, imprisoned, and nearly driven insane precisely because of her strength. . . .

Celie's Submissiveness

On the way to making Celie happy, Walker portrays her as a victim of many imaginable abuses and a few unimaginable ones. Celie is a woman who *believes* she is ugly, and she centers that belief on her blackness. While this is not a new problem with some black women, a black woman character conceived in 1982 who is still heir to the same kinds of problems that characters had who were conceived decades earlier is problematic for me—especially since Celie makes a big deal of how ugly she believes she is. But, you may say, how can a woman affirm any standard of beauty in an environment in which men are so abusive? Allowance for the fact that Celie is "living" in the 1940s really does not gainsay the criticism about this aspect of her conception. I would say in response that Nettie was there during Celie's early years, and Nettie apparently has a rather positive conception of herself. If Celie believes her about some things, why not about others? Instead, Celie gives in to her environment with a kind of passivity that comes near to provoking screams in readers not of the spectator variety who may be guilty of caring too much about the characters. Before she can be made to be happy, Celie is forced to relive the history of many Afro-American women who found themselves in unpleasant circumstances, but few of them seem to have undergone such an intuitive devaluation of themselves; even abused Linda Brent [Harriet Ann Jacobs's pseudonym in her autobiography] found some source for valuing herself, as did many women in the South who were treated as beasts of burden, but who refused to see themselves as mules of the world. I can imagine Celie existing forever in her situation if someone else did not come along to "stir her root life," as [Harlem Renaissance writer] Jean Toomer would say, "and teach her to dream." It is that burying away of the instinctive desire to save one's self that makes me in part so angry about Celie—in addition to all those ugly things that happen to her. Plowing a man's fields for twenty years and letting him use her body as a sperm depository leaves Celie so buried away from herself that it is hard to imagine anything stirring her to life—just as it is equally hard to imagine her being so deadened. Ah—the dilemma.

Celie does have an awareness of right and wrong that comes from outside herself—as well as the one she will develop from her own experiences. She knows that Albert's abuse of her is wrong just as she knew her stepfather's sexual exploitation of her was wrong. And she does go to church; whether or not she believes what she hears, certainly something of the Christian philosophy seeps into her consciousness over the years. There are guidelines for action, therefore, to which she can compare her own situation and respond. Also, considering the fact that she cannot have children with Albert, the traditional reason for enduring abuse—one's children—is absent in her case. So why does she stay? . . .

Examining the Male Identity

In classroom discussion, I discovered that *The Color Purple* is one of the most provocative works that can be offered to students. . . .

One student, older, married, and with a child of his own, told me after class one day that he couldn't read the book because of its portrayal of sexual abuse. When he finally got beyond his initial moral repugnance, he became the center of several discussions. His responses were especially important to me because he was the most articulate of the black males in the class. How Walker had presented them—or failed to present them, from his point of view—gave him several days of intellectual exercise.

This student maintained that Walker had very deliberately deprived all the black male characters in the novel of any positive identity. From giving Albert a blank instead of a name, to having the only supportive males be young and pot-heads or middle-aged and henpecked (as is the husband of Sofia's sister, for whom Celie makes a pair of pants and whose only goal in life seems to be to please his wife—because she can beat him up?), to giving [author W.E.B.] Du Bois' last name a different spelling, this student thought black men had been stripped of their identities and thus their abilities to assume the roles of men. And consider the case of poor Harpo, who doesn't even realize when he has a good thing and loses it because he has such warped notions of manhood. No man in the novel is respectable, this student maintained, not even Albert (because he can only change in terms of doing things that are traditionally considered sissified, such as sewing and gossiping). And what about the good preacher who goes off to Africa, I asked him. He's not an exception, either, the response came back, because he must get down on his knees and ask a woman for permission to get married. All the men, the student concluded, fit into that froglike perception Celie has of them. And the problem with these frogs? None of them can turn into princes. . . .

Betrayed by Its Fairy-Tale Form

The fabulist/fairy-tale mold of the novel is ultimately incongruous with and does not serve well to frame its message. When things turn out happily in those traditional tales, we are asked to affirm the basic pattern and message: Good triumphs over evil. But what does *The Color Purple* affirm? What were all those women who applauded approving of? It affirms, first of all, patience and long-suffering—perhaps to a greater degree than that exhibited by Cinderella or by the likes of Elizabeth Grimes in James Baldwin's *Go Tell It on the Mountain*. In true fairy-tale fashion, it affirms passivity; heroines in those tales do little to help themselves. It affirms silence in the face of, if not actual allegiance to, cruelty. It affirms secrecy concerning violence and violation. It affirms, saddest of all, the myth of the American Dream becoming a reality for black Americans, even those who are "dirt poor," as one of my colleagues phrased it, and those who are the "downest" and "outest." The fable structure thereby perpetuates a lie in holding out to blacks a non-existent or minimally existent hope for a piece of that great American pie. The clash of characters who presumably contend with and in the real world with the idealistic, suprarealistic quality and expectations of fairy-tale worlds places a burden on the novel that diffuses its message and guarantees possibilities for unintended interpretations.

With its mixture of message, form, and character, *The Color Purple* reads like a political shopping list of all the IOUs ["I owe yous"] Walker felt that it was time to repay. She pays homage to the feminists by portraying a woman who struggles through adversity to assert herself against almost impossible odds. She pays homage to the lesbians by portraying a relationship between two women that reads like a schoolgirl fairy tale in its ultimate adherence to the convention of the happy resolution. She pays homage to black nationalists by opposing colonialism, and to Pan Africanism by suggesting that yes, indeed, a black American does understand and sympathize with the plight of her black brothers and sisters thousands of miles across the ocean. And she adds in a few other obeisances [gestures of respect]—to career-minded women in the characters of Mary Agnes and Shug, to born-again male feminists in the character of Albert, and to black culture generally in the use of the blues and the folk idiom. . . .

A Plea for Independent-Minded Criticism

I *will* teach *The Color Purple* again—precisely because of the teachability engendered by its controversiality. I will be angry again because I am not a spectator to what happens to Celie; for me, the novel *demands* participation. I will continue to react to all praise of the novel by asserting that mere praise ignores the responsibility that goes along with it—we must clarify as much as we can the reasons that things are being praised and enumerate as best we can the consequences of that praise. I will continue to read and reread the novel, almost in self-defense against the continuing demands for discussions and oral evaluations of it. Perhaps—and other black women may share this response—I am caught in a love/hate relationship with *The Color Purple*; though my crying out against it might be comparable to spitting into a whirlwind in an effort to change its course, I shall nevertheless purse my lips.

Contemporary Perspectives on Women's Issues

Women Achieve Social Change Through Folk Art

Anne Constable

Anne Constable is a writer for the Santa Fe New Mexican, *a daily newspaper in Santa Fe, New Mexico.*

In the following viewpoint Constable introduces the village of Umoja Uaso in Kenya, founded in 1990 by a group of women abandoned by their husbands and families. Despite social and cultural obstacles, Umoja Uaso and other similar female cooperatives have thrived economically on the sale of their traditional art, after they learned to keep the men from stealing their profits. With the economic power they were able to gain, they have been able to draw attention to such social problems as domestic violence, rape, poverty, and female genital mutilation. Their progress becomes obvious every summer in Santa Fe, New Mexico, where groups from around the world gather at the Santa Fe International Folk Art Market to display and sell their artwork.

Twenty years ago [around 1990] Rebecca Lolosoli and a group of other Samburu women who had been thrown out of their homes in Kenya by their husbands and families were destitute. Some were dying of malaria. They owned nothing and couldn't afford to feed their children. "We had nobody to depend on to make our lives," Lolosoli said.

The women started brewing spirits (*changá*). But then they got arrested by police and sent hundreds of miles away. Some of their children, who were left behind, were eaten by hyenas.

Lolosoli tried to talk about these injustices during a Kenyatta Day rally [to celebrate Kenya's independence], but was shouted down.

In 1990, she and 16 others founded the village of Umoja Uaso and began pooling their money to buy supplies for making jewelry which they sold on the street.

"We wanted to uplift our lives," Lolosoli said.

But once the men saw that a woman had sold something, "they would take the money and beat them," she said. Today the women are careful not to keep much cash around and earnings are quickly deposited in a bank account. "We never give (the men) our money because they just want it to go and get drunk," Lolosoli explained.

Women Transform Their Communities

Now the members of Umoja Uaso Women's Group No. 48 . . . [are] still fighting for their rights—"Men don't want to see women having anything." From sales of their brightly colored beaded jewelry they've built a pre-school, provided shelter for women who have been beaten and raped and paid hospital fees for their group from a special fund. Lolosoli also talks to villagers about female genital mutilation. Last year [2009] during a drought in the area, they bought food and water to share with neighboring villages using revenues earned from the Santa Fe [New Mexico] International Folk Art Market.

"That money really saved so many people," Lolosoli said.

Umoja Uaso is one of 10 women's cooperatives featured in a new exhibit at the Santa Fe International Folk Art Museum called "Empowering Women: Artisan Cooperatives That Transform Communities."

The exhibit in the Museum of International Folk Art's "Gallery of Conscience" is the first in a series exploring the challenges faced by 21st-century folk artists.

Museum director Marsha Bol asked Suzanne Seriff, a folklorist at the University of Texas, to curate the show. Seriff

Every summer, groups from across the world display and sell their artwork at the Santa Fe International Folk Art Market. © David Moore/Alamy.

chose 10 jointly owned and democratically controlled women's cooperatives from among the 40 or so that had applied to the 2010 Santa Fe International Folk Art Market. The groups represent Swaziland, South Africa, Nepal, Lao PDR [People's Democratic Republic], India, Peru, Bolivia, Morocco, Kenya and Rwanda.

Seriff was already working with the market developing the process for selecting artists among the hundreds who apply.

Most cooperatives fail, Seriff said, because the members can't find consistent access to markets, or they don't share the same vision. But others across the globe have made profound differences in their communities by investing in education, health and the environment.

Traditional Art and Social Change

For the show, Seriff said she wanted to do more than exhibit a bunch of beautiful things from around the world. She wanted to focus on how women were fighting things like domestic violence, rape, suicide, hunger and war through their traditional art.

In many cases, they are struggling to keep their arts alive. "The next generation is moving to the cities and doing sex work," Seriff said. "Weaving baskets is not what they're into."

Each of the co-ops sent a sample piece for the exhibit—although not necessarily their most elaborate or difficult work.

Weavers from OckPopTok, a cooperative founded 10 years ago by a London fashion photographer and the daughter of a master weaver from the Mekong region of the Lao People's Democratic Republic, made a silk wall hanging that looks like a traditional prayer flag but incorporates contemporary weaving designs. The co-op, which grew from a one-room studio to a gallery retreat center and collaborative for more than 200 artisans, is now teaching the children of the weavers how to create designs on a computer.

Cheque Oitedie Cooperative in Bolivia submitted an example of a bag woven from the fiber of a bromeliad [a succulent plant of the pineapple family], garabatá fino. Inés Hinojosa Ossio, an ethnobotanist, is working with the indigenous women to sustainably raise the plant in a new location. Thirty years ago, the Ayoreo community was forcibly relocated by missionaries seeking to "civilize" them, and the tribe found that the plant they used was almost nonexistent in their new home.

"The women are closely linked with this plant," Hinojosa said. And now they are able to sell their bags in the international market at higher prices. (Each bag takes three weeks to make, and the women previously were earning about $20 a bag.) At the market, she said, "Prices are better, and this is a good opportunity to maintain the culture."

From Rwanda come "peace baskets," woven from sisal, sweetgrass, papyrus, reeds, bamboo and other materials by female survivors of the 1994 genocide, which left a million people dead and hundreds of thousands of widows and orphans.

In the refugee camps, where Janet Nkubana grew up, the women took up their old culture of weaving baskets—when they weren't cooking and cleaning. The baskets were traditionally used to present food and gifts, "to give them more respect," she said.

Nkubana wondered how the women could turn weaving into a business opportunity. She helped found Gahaya Links Cooperative, which has grown from 20 women to 52 co-ops and more than 4,000 weavers—both Hutus and rival Tutsis [Rwandan tribes]—across the country. Their baskets are sold at Macy's, and the Clinton Global Initiative bought 400 of them.

As a result of earnings from [2009's] market in Santa Fe, Nkubana said, four women bought cows, two put electricity in their houses and many bought goats, pigs and rabbits to raise.

Domestic Violence Retains Cultural Momentum Worldwide

Sonya Weakley

Sonya Weakley writes for American.gov, *a publication of the US State Department's Bureau of International Information Programs.*

According to Weakley in this article, social and cultural attitudes have been found to encourage violence against women around the world. One out of three women worldwide are abused, she reports. In the modern small family, as opposed to the old-fashioned extended family, abused women often have no one to turn to. In Weakley's view, abuse appears in cycles: the father of an abuser is often an abuser himself. Abuse of women is so ingrained in society that the victims blame themselves and are too afraid to testify, she maintains. Abuse is rooted in the idea of gender inequality and the power and control of males, Weakley says, and addressing the issue effectively is hindered by the ingrained attitudes of the police. The author explains that many organizations employ a multipronged approach to domestic violence: they provide medical, psychological, and legal services to victims; bring global attention to the issues of gender inequity and abuse; and train law enforcement and judicial agencies.

Aissata Cisse is a pediatrician in Africa, but many of her patients are adult women. While practicing in Niger and most recently in Senegal, Cisse saw women who were abused by their husbands or intimate partners. These women were trying to take care of their children, but she knew they needed help first.

Cisse realized she would have to provide several services to the women, so she organized a group of specialists that could provide various services, including legal and psychological. "I counsel women, listen to them, and I give advice. It is my job."

Cultural and Economic Factors

She knows that in most cases, the woman is the victim of a man whose father abused [the man's] mother. "It is a cycle, and it will continue," she said, eventually affecting the children of the mother who shows up at [Cisse's] door.

In 1999, The United Nations General Assembly designated November 25 as the International Day for the Elimination of Violence Against Women.

In remarks to the UN Commission on the Status of Women in February 2008, UN Secretary-General Ban Ki-moon said at least one out of three women in the world is likely to be beaten, coerced into sex or otherwise abused in her lifetime.

"Violence against women is an issue that cannot wait," he said. "No country, no culture, no woman young or old is immune to this scourge."

Cisse, who recently came to the United States to get a master's degree in public health, believes domestic violence stems from cultural and economic factors, such as a trend toward smaller families.

A May 2008 United Nations report cites a worldwide shift from extended families to nuclear families. Cisse says she has seen this change leave abused women with no one to turn to, and with no one to hold the abuser accountable.

According to the 2006 United Nations report titled *In-Depth Study on All Forms of Violence against Women*, such cultural barriers are common. "Male violence against women is generated by socio-cultural attitudes and cultures of violence in all parts of the world, and especially by norms about the control of female reproduction and sexuality."

International Fight Against Domestic Abuse

Numerous government and nongovernmental organizations throughout the world are working to end domestic violence, according to the UN report. The United States assists countries through grants from the US Department of Justice, the US Agency for International Development, the US Department of State and others.

One of the priorities is to train law enforcement agencies and courts to recognize the problem and treat it appropriately. The training also helps break down social barriers, according to judges and lawyers who have worked directly with police officers, prosecutors, judges and legislators outside the US.

Susan Block, a retired circuit court judge in St. Louis, [Missouri,] has traveled to Lithuania, among other countries, to train judges and help them develop civil protection orders that would be enforceable within the system. She also has helped prosecutors come up with ways to prosecute without the victim's testimony, as some victims are reluctant to testify against their abusers.

She gave police officers ideas for tactics, such as using "excitable utterances" as evidence even if the victim is not in court. "If the woman called an emergency number or said excitable things to police, the police officer could use it."

She found younger police officers most receptive. "They said they became police officers to help people, and they were anxious to do something about this."

Wanda Lucibello, a special-victims prosecutor in New York, has hosted many international delegations and traveled to many countries, including Grenada, Belize, South Africa and Zimbabwe, to provide training.

Because Lucibello works with one of several family justice centers sponsored by the US Justice Department around the

United States, she often presents the justice center model—providing many services in one place—in other countries.

In some countries, she finds gender inequality "so powerful. It is an additional hurdle to get through." She also finds that some of her trainees have had personal experiences with domestic violence within their own families, or they recognize some of the characteristics in themselves.

Complications with Prosecution

In many cases, her international training involves helping police and prosecutors take domestic violence seriously, but often she finds more distress than resistance.

"They share the same frustrations and concerns as police officers [in the United States]," such as the victim not wanting to press charges against the abuser.

She also offers ideas for successful prosecution. "I compare it to gathering evidence as though they were handling an arrest for a homicide, [in that] there is no victim [from whom to obtain information]. That gets them excited because they [then] have a way of looking at it."

Judge Ramona Gonzales of the La Crosse County, Wisconsin, Circuit Court has taught "Domestic Violence 101" in Guam and other places.

"We tell them what they need to be sensitive to and what questions to ask—has the victim been isolated from her family and friends?"

She stresses that domestic violence goes beyond the physical attack. "It is about power and control." The fear, she said, is that the controlling behavior won't reach the judicial system "until you have a homicide or suicide or both."

Conflicting Feminist Ideologies Among Black Women

Patricia Hill Collins

Patricia Hill Collins is Distinguished University Professor of Sociology at the University of Maryland. Her books include Fighting Words: Black Women's Search for Justice *and* Black Feminist Thought.

In this selection Collins writes that the term womanism *is a somewhat exclusionary word describing black feminists who are in conflict with feminists of other races. In recent years, she explains, differences have developed between black feminism and womanism. Womanists have come to distance themselves from white feminists, who are regarded as being part of the white enemy. They tend to see their problem in terms of race, and they see womanism as a way to work for the betterment of black women without attacking black men. In Collins's view, the agenda of white feminists is simply not the same. Black feminism, on the other hand, is more concerned with confronting oppressive men and male cultures throughout the world to demand justice and equality for women. Even as black feminists fight for the rights of black women globally, the author claims, they are more inclined to work with white feminists.*

As [African American scholar] Barbara Omolade points out, "black feminism is sometimes referred to as womanism because both are concerned with struggles against sexism and racism by black women who are themselves part of the black community's efforts to achieve equity and liberty."

Patricia Hill Collins, "What's in a Name? Womanism, Black Feminism, and Beyond," *The Black Scholar*, vol. 26, 1996. Copyright © 1996 by The Black Scholar. Reproduced by permission.

But despite similar beliefs expressed by African American women who define themselves as black feminists, as womanists, as both, or, in some cases, as neither, increasing attention seems devoted to delineating the differences, if any, between groups naming themselves as "womanists" or "black feminists." The *name* given to black women's collective standpoint seems to matter, but why?

In this paper, I explore some of the theoretical implications of using the terms "womanism" and "black feminism" to name a black woman's standpoint. My purpose is not to classify either the works of black women or African American women themselves into one category or the other. Rather, I aim to examine how the effort to categorize obscures more basic challenges that confront African American women as a group. . . .

Womanism and Racial Separation

Womanism offers a distance from the "enemy," in this case, whites generally and white women in particular, yet still raises the issue of gender. Due to its endorsement of racial separatism, this interpretation of womanism offers a vocabulary for addressing gender issues within African American communities without challenging the racially segregated terrain that characterizes American social institutions.

This use of womanism sidesteps an issue central to many white feminists, namely, finding ways to foster interracial cooperation among women. African American women embracing black nationalist philosophies typically express little interest in working with white women—in fact, white women are defined as part of the problem. Moreover, womanism appears to provide an avenue to foster stronger relationships between black women and black men, another very important issue for African American women regardless of political perspective. . . . Many black women view feminism as a movement that, at best, is exclusively for women and, at worst, dedicated to attacking or eliminating men. [African American poet] Sherley Williams takes this view when she notes that in contrast to feminism, "womanist inquiry . . . assumes that it can talk both effectively and productively about men." Womanism seemingly supplies a way for black women to address gender oppression without attacking black men. . . .

A Growing Ethical System

This meaning of womanism seems rooted in another major political tradition within African American politics, namely, a pluralist version of black empowerment. Pluralism views society as being composed of various ethnic and interest groups, all of whom compete for goods and services. Equity lies in providing equal opportunities, rights, and respect to all groups. By retaining black cultural distinctiveness and integrity, pluralism offers a modified version of racial integration premised not on individual assimilation but on *group* integration. Clearly rejecting what they perceive as being the limited vision of feminism projected by North American white women, many black women theorists have been attracted to this joining of pluralism and racial integration in this interpretation of [Alice] Walker's "womanism." For example, black feminist theologian Katie Geneva Cannon's (1988) work *Black Womanist Ethics* invokes this sense of the visionary content of womanism. As an ethical system, womanism is always in the making—it is not a closed, fixed system of ideas but one that continually evolves through its rejection of all forms of oppression and commitment to social justice. . . .

[One] significant feature of black women's multiple uses of womanism concerns the potential for a slippage between the real and the ideal. To me, there is a distinction between describing black women's historical responses to racial and gender oppression as being womanist, and using womanism as a visionary term delineating an ethical or ideal vision of humanity for all people. Identifying the liberatory *potential* within black women's communities that emerges from concrete, historical experiences remains quite different from claiming that black women have already *arrived* at this ideal, "womanist" endpoint. Refusing to distinguish carefully between these two meanings of womanism thus collapses the historically real and the future ideal into one privileged position for African American women in the present. Taking this position is reminiscent of the response of some black women to the admittedly narrow feminist agenda forwarded by white women in the early 1970s. Those black women proclaimed that they were already "liberated" while in actuality, this was far from the truth.

Black Feminism in the Global Context

African American women who use the term black feminism also attach varying interpretations to this term. As black feminist theorist and activist Pearl Cleage defines it, feminism is "the belief that women are full human beings capable of participation and leadership in the full range of human activities—intellectual, political, social, sexual, spiritual and economic." In its broadest sense, feminism constitutes both an ideology and a global political movement that confronts sexism, a social relationship in which males as a group have authority over females as a group.

Globally, a feminist agenda encompasses several major areas. First and foremost, the economic status of women and issues associated with women's global poverty, such as educational opportunities, industrial development, environmental racism, employment policies, prostitution, and inheritance laws concerning property, constitute a fundamental global women's issue. Political rights for women, such as gaining the vote, rights of assembly, traveling in public, officeholding, the rights of political prisoners, and basic human rights violations against women such as rape and torture constitute a second area of concern. A third area of global concern consists of marital and family issues such as marriage and divorce laws, child custody policies, and domestic labor. Women's health and survival issues, such as reproductive rights, pregnancy, sexuality, and AIDS constitute another area of global feminist concern. This broad global feminist agenda finds varying expressions in different regions of the world and among diverse populations.

Using the term "black feminism" positions African American women to examine how the particular constellation of issues affecting black women in the United States are part of issues of women's emancipation struggles globally. In the context of feminism as a global political movement for women's rights and emancipation, the patterns of feminist knowledge and politics that African American women encounter in the United States represent but a narrow segment refracted through the dichotomous racial politics of white supremacy in the United States. Because the media in the United States portrays feminism as a for-whites-only movement, and because many white women have accepted this view of American apartheid that leads to segregated institutions of all types, including feminist organizations, feminism is often viewed by both black and whites as the cultural property of white women.

Race and Gender Divided

Despite their media erasure, many African American women have long struggled against this exclusionary feminism and have long participated in what appear to be for-whites-only feminist activity. In some cases, some black women have long directly challenged the racism within feminist organizations controlled by white women. [African American abolitionist and women's rights activist] Sojourner Truth's often cited phrase "ain't I a woman" typifies this long-standing tradition. At other times, even though black women's participation in feminist organizations remains largely invisible, for example,

[African American feminist] Pauli Murray's lack of recognition as a founding member of NOW [National Organization for Women], black women participated in feminist organizations in positions of leadership. In still other cases, black women combine allegedly divergent political agendas. For example, Pearl Cleage observes that black feminist politics and black nationalist politics need not be contradictory. She notes, "I don't think you can be a true Black Nationalist, dedicated to the freedom of black people *without* being a feminist, black *people* being made up of both men and *women*, after all, and feminism being nothing more or less than a belief in the political, social and legal equality of women."

Using the term "black feminism" disrupts the racism inherent in presenting feminism as a for-whites-only ideology and political movement. Inserting the adjective "black" challenges the assumed whiteness of feminism and disrupts the false universal of this term for both white and black women. Since many white women think that black women lack feminist consciousness, the term "black feminist" both highlights the contradictions underlying the assumed whiteness of feminism and serves to remind white women that they comprise neither the only nor the normative "feminists." The term "black feminism" also makes many African American women uncomfortable because it challenges black women to confront their own views on sexism and women's oppression. Because the majority of African American women encounter their own experiences repackaged in racist school curricula and media, even though they may support the very ideas on which feminism rests, large numbers of African American women reject the term "feminism" because of what they perceive as its association with whiteness. Many see feminism as operating exclusively within the terms white and American and perceive its opposite as being black and American. When given these two narrow and false choices, black women routinely choose "race" and let the lesser question of "gender" go. . . .

The Limitations of a Label

Several difficulties accompany the use of the term "black feminism." One involves the problem of balancing the genuine concerns of black women against continual pressures to absorb and recast such interests within white feminist frameworks. For example, ensuring political rights and economic development via collective action to change social institutions remains a strong focal point in the feminism of African American women and women of color. Yet the emphasis on themes such as personal identity, understanding "difference," deconstructing women's multiple selves, and the simplistic model of the political expressed through the slogan the "personal is political," that currently permeate North American white women's feminism in the academy can work to sap black feminism of its critical edge. Efforts of contemporary black women thinkers to explicate a long-standing black women's intellectual tradition bearing the label "black feminism" can attract the attention of white women armed with a different feminist agenda. . . .

No term currently exists that adequately represents the substance of what diverse groups of black women alternately call "womanism" and "black feminism." Perhaps the time has come to go beyond naming by applying main ideas contributed by both womanists and black feminists to the overarching issue of analyzing the centrality of gender in shaping a range of relationships within African American communities.

A Black Celebrity Decides to Make Her Sexual Orientation Known

Ari Karpel

Writer and editor Ari Karpel is a regular contributor to the Ad-
vocate, the New York Times, *and the* Los Angeles Times.

In this selection Karpel writes about an interview with Wanda
Sykes, a black comedian and actor who came out as a lesbian in
late 2008. Sykes opens up to Karpel about some details of her
struggle with sexual identity, her failed heterosexual marriage,
and her current marriage to a woman. Karpel promotes the im-
portance of Sykes's coming out for the African American commu-
nity in particular because of the stigma still associated with gays
and lesbians. But, Karpel insists, Sykes draws a firm line between
her public and private lives, and she explains the added dimen-
sion of "coming out" for celebrities.

When Wanda Sykes strolled onstage at the Trevor Project's
[a suicide and crisis prevention helpline for gay and
questioning youth] annual Cracked Xmas fund-raiser last De-
cember [2008] in Los Angeles, the crowd leapt to its feet in a
standing ovation. After the applause and whoops subsided the
comedian quipped, "Oh, come on, it ain't like you never seen
a black lesbian before."

In a sense, they hadn't. While well-known actors like T.R.
Knight and Neil Patrick Harris have come out of the closet in
recent years without breaking the stride of their mainstream
careers, African-Americans have been conspicuously absent
from the parade of "Yep, I'm Gay" magazine covers [referring
to *Time* magazine's cover of Ellen DeGeneres when she came

out]. And when the 44-year-old comedian told a Las Vegas rally on November 15 that she and her wife had been married just weeks earlier, it was the first time anyone outside Hollywood and Sykes's circle of friends and family knew for sure that she was gay. "When California passed Prop. 8 . . . I felt like I was being personally attacked, our community was attacked," she said. "They pissed off the wrong group of people!"[1]

Onstage—and on [television show] *Curb Your Enthusiasm*—Sykes is the angry loudmouth, hilariously outraged at the injustices of the world. Her trademark is her voice, which always rises as she spits out expletives to expertly cut through any bull that sparks her anger—whether it's directed at former president George W. Bush ("Either he's retarded or he thinks we're retarded") or people who oppose marriage equality ("Why do you care that Bob and Jim are getting married, unless you were planning on f---ing Bob or Jim?").

Promoting Gay Rights in Public

With that mouth, you'd think Sykes would have come out of the closet a long time ago, and as far as she's concerned, she did. She's performed at gay pride festivals and on the True Colors Tour—and even did stand-up aboard a gay cruise. She also shot a public-service announcement for the Gay, Lesbian, and Straight Education Network last year [2008] and spoke out against California's Proposition 8 on the *Ellen* show a week before the election. But with all her shtick about her ex-husband and their failed marriage ("We were married seven years, no kids. So we went out of business. No inventory"), her fans can be forgiven for assuming that Sykes was a well-meaning straight ally. After all, her straight *New Adventures of Old Christine* costar Julia Louis-Dreyfus also spoke out against Prop. 8 on *Ellen* (and in this magazine [the *Advocate*])—not that there's anything wrong with that.

1. In November 2008, ballot Proposition 8—which states that "only marriage between a man and a woman is valid or recognized in California"—overturned the California Supreme Court's ruling to the contrary.

Entertainer Wanda Sykes announced she was a lesbian in 2008. Her coming out was an important event for the African American community. Getty Images.

Now that she's out of the closet, what kind of lesbian spokeswoman will Sykes be? Will the take-no-prisoners ferocity of her Comedy Central and HBO specials be put to use on behalf of her fellow gay people? Will she be the in-your-face Rosie O'Donnell of African-American gays? Or will she be the more aw-shucks Ellen DeGeneres type? With anger running high among gays over blacks' perceived opposition to marriage equality and with only a handful of high-profile African-Americans out in Hollywood, will Sykes be the healing link between two simmering worlds?

Sitting down for her first—and, she says, only—significant interview about her coming-out, Sykes is soft-spoken almost to the point of being subdued. Nursing a midday glass of wine at Smokehouse, a restaurant across the street from the Warner Bros. studio where *Old Christine* is shot, she's reluctant to open up about her personal life. Granting this interview has put her in the position of being asked questions she's not sure she wants to answer—questions like "When did you realize you were a lesbian?" and "Why did your first marriage end?"

"This is weird," she complains. "This is for *The Advocate*, right?" Right. "So why do you need to know this stuff? Isn't it just preaching to the choir?"

Sykes may be uneasy getting personal, but she has a firm grasp on why it's important for an African-American celebrity to help normalize homosexuality. "There's such a stigma about being gay that a lot of the men don't want to be labeled as gay, so they live straight lives, and then, behind closed doors, they're fooling around with men, bringing HIV home to their wives," she says, stepping confidently onto a soapbox. "We're literally killing ourselves over this fear of homosexuality." In an effort to address these issues and "build this bridge" between gays and blacks, Sykes joined the board of Equality California in November [2008]. "One of the things that's so terrific about Wanda is she's not rushing out there to be the face of anything," says Geoff Kors, the gay rights organization's executive director. "She actually wanted to figure out how she could roll up her sleeves and get involved, to come to board meetings, to engage in dialogue to change hearts and minds."

So far, Sykes is still finding her voice as an activist. But if her history is any indication, there's little doubt she'll end up saying whatever she feels. . . .

Sykes Wrestled with Her Sexual Identity

Just before moving to New York [from the Washington, D.C., area], Sykes married record producer David Hall. "I actually made the choice to be straight as a kid," she says. "Early on I knew [being gay] wasn't gonna fly. No way. And from the teachers and church and all it was, This is wrong! What's wrong with me? And you pray and ask God to take it away, and you bury it and bury it, and you shut that part of yourself off. Then you try to live the life that you've supposed to live."

She and Hall divorced in 1998, but Sykes is careful to clarify that her marriage didn't end because of her sexual orientation. "It had nothing to do with that. My marriage was fine. I think it was just . . . I don't want to get too much into that." She hesitates, and then continues, "It's just that when you bury a part of yourself, you can take those relationships only so far because you can't be totally open. Once we were divorced there was a defining, liberating moment of, OK, I'm free of this marriage, now what? It's kind of like giving yourself permission. I guess that's when I started actively dating women."

In 2006, Sykes went on a weeklong, end-of-summer vacation with friends to Cherry Grove, one of two predominantly gay communities on New York's Fire Island. ("I'm not making that Pines money," she says of the neighboring, ritzier enclave, Fire Island Pines. "But it's so nice over at the Pines. Nice coffee shops, gourmet foods, and all that crap over there.") It was a nasty, rainy day, but on the ferry ride to the island Sykes spotted an intriguing woman. "She had on this black trench coat and was carrying a computer bag," she says. "I was like, We're going to Fire Island—what the hell is she doing with her laptop?"

It wasn't so much the trench coat or the laptop, though, that sparked Sykes's attention. "She just caught my eye," she says. And that's when something happened that she'd never experienced before. "It was like a voice inside me saying, See? That's what you need, Wanda. That's what you need." Sykes's eyes well up with tears as she tells the story. "She's beautiful, but there was just this aura about her. We've been inseparable since." Inseparable and protective: Sykes, walking a tightrope, will not say what her wife does for a living. In fact, she tells the whole story of their meeting without once uttering her wife's name. Later Sykes decided to give us her first name, Alexandra, for the article. "She's not in show business. I want her to have as much of her private life as she can."

Legal Implications for a Lesbian Couple

Two years later, emboldened by the California supreme court's ruling in favor of marriage equality, she and Alexandra decided to make it official. "This was it," Sykes explains. "We're in love and we want to spend the rest of our lives together. That's why you get married." So they rented a small hotel in Palm Springs and were married in a simple ceremony before about 40 friends and family members. "We had an amazing weekend. I don't like to talk about it. It was a very special moment for us, for our friends. I like to keep that." Sykes is happy—and obviously sentimental: "Even looking at the pictures, I just go back to that moment and get all teary-eyed."

On November 4, still riding high on the joy of their recent nuptials, Sykes and Alexandra were lifted even higher at the news of Barack Obama's [presidential election] victory. But just a few hours later, like so many progressive Californians, they experienced emotional whiplash as it became evident that Prop. 8 had passed.

As an African-American in a week-old marriage, it stung Sykes even more when reports started coming in that black voters had overwhelmingly sided with the antigay measure. (Initial reports that 70% of African-Americans voters supported Prop. 8 have recently been debunked; a National Gay and Lesbian Task Force Policy Institute study has shown that a more accurate number is 57%–59%.) She said it felt as if her family was being attacked. "Like, hey I'm sitting here living my life and suddenly the government—the people, really—walked in the door to our living room and said, 'No, you're not allowed to do this.' And that's frightening."

At first, the comedian says, she felt guilty and wondered if she should have been more outspoken. "I mean, I wrote the checks and signed the petitions and did all that, but could I have done more?" Then she realized that, for her, doing more would mean one thing: coming out publicly. It was a wake-up call, she says. "Now I have to be in your face." So, that night, she and Alexandra discussed it. "I said, 'This is what I feel I have to do,' and she was totally supportive. She was like, 'OK, let's do this.'" The next morning, Sykes called someone she'd met years before but barely knew—out gay actor Doug Spearman ([from cable series] Noah's Arc), who is African-American and who, as Sykes remembered, served on Equality California's board of directors.

"I had no idea Wanda was gay," Spearman says today. "But she is a huge hero of mine—as an actress, as a comedian, and as a working black person." Perhaps that's why he didn't believe it really was Sykes who'd left him a voice mail that morning. "I thought, Somebody's playing a little tricky trick on me."

Career Vulnerability for a Lesbian Actress

But Sykes persisted, texting and telephoning Spearman until the two finally spoke and planned to meet for lunch, where Sykes told him she was ready to come out publicly. Right away, Spearman says, he expressed concern for Sykes's career. "As much as I'd like to be Sean Penn playing Harvey Milk saying, 'You must come out, you must come out,' everyone has to do what's right for them," he says. "And I told her [that coming out] has huge ramifications for your career. If you do anything that makes people in Hollywood say 'I can't hire you,' you're taking a big risk."

But Sykes had already thought that through. Plenty of comedians are out of the closet, she argued. And besides, she never gets cast as the love interest anyway. Whether she's playing the sassy aide to Steve Carell's congressman (*Evan Almighty*), the long-suffering assistant to Jane Fonda's veteran news anchor (*Monster-in-Law*), or Luke Wilson's mouthy boss (*My Super Ex-Girlfriend*), Sykes always plays the single black woman. "People really don't think of me in a sexual context," she says matter-of-factly. "They don't look at Wanda Sykes and think sex."

Sykes was scheduled to perform at Planet Hollywood in Las Vegas the weekend of November 15, when post-Prop. 8 rallies were planned at city halls and statehouses across the country, and she intended to attend the local demonstration with friends. She'd gone to marches in Los Angeles in the days immediately following the election, but no one paid much attention to her. Las Vegas was a different story, though. Just when Sykes thought the speeches were over and people were preparing to march, one of the event's organizers announced, "There's a rumor Wanda Sykes is out there." So, as she'd done thousands of times before, Sykes jumped onto the stage. Only this time, she told no jokes and used no profanity.

"It was from the heart," she says today of her speech. "I just said what I said; I don't really talk about my sexual orientation. I wasn't in the closet, but I was just living my life. Everybody who knows me personally knows I'm gay. And that's the way people should be able to live their lives, really. We shouldn't have to be standing out here demanding something we automatically should have as citizens of this country." She ended the impromptu presentation with a statement of pride: "I'm proud to be a woman, I'm proud to be a black woman, and I'm proud to be gay. Let's go get our damn equal rights."

By the time she'd returned to her hotel room, news that Sykes had come out of the closet was on the CNN [news] crawl. "I was like, Damn, whatever happened to 'What happens in Vegas . . . ?'"

Juggling Issues of Race, Gender, and Sexual Identity

Sykes resists the notion that she might become some sort of poster child. "I can only give you my perspective, and I don't represent all black lesbians," she says, a little defensively. "Right now my attention is equal rights for the gay community because personally that's the one that's really affecting me right now. I'm sure as I get more involved I'll see the [racial] divide and that's when I'll go, 'Oh, my God, that's f---ed up. Why is there this divide?'"

For someone accustomed to years of suppressing her sexual orientation, it seems natural to compartmentalize identities. But she's quick to point out that it's easy—and dangerous—to generalize about any group of people. "[African-Americans] are not all this homogenous group. If you live in your little community and you don't know gay people and you don't know that we're loving people and we all want the same things, then you won't be able to identify with them or care about that other group." And she's more diplomatic than her stand-up persona might suggest: "Speaking from the people I know," she says, "it's tougher for a black person to come out [than it is for someone who's white]. Then again, I'm sure there's some white people from the Bible Belt who have been disowned from their families and have had a hard time."

Sykes's longtime friend Chris Rock puts it more bluntly: "It's harder being black, and it's harder being a woman.

Everything's harder if you're black. It's harder chewing gum," he quips. And Nadine Smith, executive director of the gay rights organization Equality Florida, believes that humor will ultimately be Sykes's most important tool: "What Wanda most needs to continue to do is be funny and draw audiences and find the innovative and clever ways she always has to drop some knowledge on people and open their minds." That said, Sykes also doesn't intend to become a "lesbian comedian." "I can't do that," she says. "I'm still me. I was born a lesbian, I just didn't talk about it, so there's always been that perspective."

Coming Out for a Celebrity

"She's a private person," says her costar Louis-Dreyfus. "So [coming out] was a big decision for her. I'm proud of her." Even at work, among friends, Sykes keeps personal information to herself. On the weekend Sykes got married, Louis-Dreyfus called to invite the couple over for a game night. "She said, 'I can't, I'm out of town,'" Louis-Dreyfus says. "She didn't even tell me she was getting married! That's how private she is."

It's not that she's trying to be secretive, Sykes says: "I don't shut anyone out, but I'm not overly open." As far as she's concerned, she's been out of the closet for years. "I was out at work, I was out to my family, I was out to my friends. I lived my life as a lesbian," she says. "But because I'm a celebrity I have to do this additional step, which is to tell total strangers that I'm a lesbian."

Despite her annoyance at that additional step, the past few months have been more meaningful than she anticipated. "I didn't know it would be this liberating," she declares. And yet there's one area in which she still has a way to go. "I hate identifying myself as a celebrity," she says, only half joking. "I'm still not there. I'm a closeted celebrity."

For Further Discussion

1. What aspects of Alice Walker's life may have contributed to her portraits of men in *The Color Purple*? Use the first chapter's selections from Maria Lauret, Evelyn C. White, and Barbara T. Christian to inform your answer.

2. How are women portrayed as being brutalized and discriminated against in this novel? Consider each of the women, not just Celie, using the selections of Donna Haisty Winchell, Martha J. Cutter, and Charles L. Proudfit in formulating your answer.

3. Describe the many reversals of gender roles in the novel and explain your understanding of why Walker used such a device and whether it was effective. Use the selections by Henry O. Dixon, Mae G. Henderson, and bell hooks as resources in your responses.

4. How is the concept of God changed in Celie's mind to accommodate women's character? Cite from the selections by Valerie Babb and Donna Haisty Winchell in forming your answer.

5. How do women's connections with one another and women's folk art help them to survive, according to Donna Haisty Winchell, Mae G. Henderson, Keith E. Byerman, and Anne Constable?

6. Do you agree with the charges of stereotyping and lack of racial concern leveled against the novel in the selections of Trudier Harris, Philip M. Royster, Keith E. Byerman, and bell hooks? Why or why not?

For Further Reading

Toni Cade Bambara, *The Salt Eater*. New York: Vintage Books, 1980.

Zora Neale Hurston, *Mules and Men*. Philadelphia: Lippincott, 1935.

Toni Morrison, *The Bluest Eye*. New York: Holt, Rinehart, and Winston, 1970.

Alice Walker, *By the Light of My Father's Smile*. New York: Random House, 1998.

———, *Meridian*. New York: Harcourt Brace, 1976.

———, *Now Is the Time to Open Your Heart: A Novel*. New York: Random House, 2004.

———, *Possessing the Secret of Joy*. New York: Harcourt, Brace, Jovanovich, 1992.

———, *The Temple of My Familiar*. San Diego: Harcourt Brace, Jovanovich, 1989.

———, *The Third Life of Grange Copeland*. New York: Harcourt, Brace, Jovanovich, 1970.

———, *The Way Forward Is with a Broken Heart*. New York: Random House, 2000.

Bibliography

Books

Gerri Bates — *Alice Walker: A Critical Companion.* Westport, CT: Greenwood, 2005.

Harold Bloom, ed. — *Alice Walker.* Updated ed. New York: Bloom's Literary Criticism, 2007.

Elliott Butler-Evans — *Race, Gender, and Desire: Narrative Strategies in the Fiction of Toni Cade Bambara, Toni Morrison, and Alice Walker.* Philadelphia: Temple University Press, 1989.

Katie Cannon — *Womanism and the Soul of the Black Community.* New York: Continuum, 1995.

Ricardo Carilo and Jerry Teleo, eds. — *Family Violence and Men of Color.* New York: Springer, 2008.

Barbara Christian — *Black Feminist Criticism: Perspectives on Black Women Writers.* New York: Pergamon, 1985.

Patricia Hill Collins — *Fighting Words: Black Women and the Search for Justice.* Minneapolis: University of Minnesota Press, 1998.

Ikenna Dieke, ed. — *Critical Essays on Alice Walker.* Westport, CT: Greenwood, 1999.

Eric Michael Dyson	"Sexual Fault Lines: Robbing Love Between Us," in *The State of Black America 2007*. New York: National Urban League, 2007.
Gail Garfield	*Knowing What We Know: African American Women's Experiences of Violence and Violation*. New Brunswick, NJ: Rutgers University Press, 2005.
Henry Louis Gates Jr. and K.A. Appiah, eds.	*Alice Walker: Critical Perspectives Past and Present*. New York: Amistad, 1993.
Tony Gentry and Nathan I Huggins	*Alice Walker: Author*. Black Americans of Achievement Series. New York: Chelsea House, 1993.
Sandra M. Gilbert	*No Man's Land: The Place of the Woman Writer in the Twentieth Century*. New Haven, CT: Yale University Press, 1988.
Kate Havelin	*Incest: Why Am I Afraid to Tell?* Mankato, MN: Life Matters, 2000.
Lillie P. Howard, ed.	*Alice Walker and Zora Neale Hurston: The Common Bond*. Westport, CT: Greenwood, 1993.
Karla Simicikova	*To Live Fully, Here and Now. The Healing Vision in the Works of Alice Walker*. New York: Lexington Books, 2007.
Carolyn M. West, ed.	*Violence in the Lives of Black Women: Battered Black and Blue*. New York: Haworth, 2002

Periodicals

Linda Abbandonato	"A View from Elsewhere: Subversive Sexuality and the Rewriting of the Heroine's Story in *The Color Purple*," *PMLA*, vol. 106, 1991.
Sandra Alps	"Concepts of Selfhood in *Their Eyes Were Watching God* and *The Color Purple*," *Pacific Review*, vol. 1, 1986.
Margaret Kent Bass	"Alice's Secret," *CLA Journal*, September 1994.
Lauren Berlant	"Race, Gender, and Nation in *The Color Purple*," *Critical Inquiry*, vol. 11, no. 1, 1988.
Jacqueline Bobo	"Sifting Through the Controversy: Reading *The Color Purple*," *Callaloo: A Journal of African America and African Arts and Letters*, vol. 12, no. 2, 1989.
Marie H. Buncombe	"Androgyny as Metaphor in Alice Walker's Novels," *CLA Journal*, June 1987.
King-Kok Cheung	"'Don't Tell': Imposed Silences in *The Color Purple* and *The Woman Warrior*," *PMLA*, March 1988.
April L. Few	"Integrating Black Consciousness and Critical Race Feminism into Family Studies Research," *Journal of Family Issues*, April 2007.

Christine Froula   "The Daughter's Seduction: Sexual
                    Violence and Literary History,"
                    SIGNS, Summer 1986.

Mimi Hall   "Women's Rights a Priority for
                    Obama Panel," *USA Today,*
                    September 13, 2009.

Trudier Harris   "From Victimization to Free
                    Enterprise: Alice Walker's *The Color
                    Purple*," *Studies in American Fiction,*
                    vol. 14, no. 1, 1986.

Om P. Juneja   "The Purple Colour of Walker
                    Women: Their Journey from Slavery
                    to Liberation," *The Literary Criterion,*
                    vol. 25, 1990.

Lori Duin Kelly   "Theology and Androgyny: The Role
                    of Religion in *The Color Purple*,"
                    Notes on Contemporary Literature,
                    vol. 18, no. 2, 1988.

Daniel W. Ross   "Celie in the Looking Glass: The
                    Desire for Selfhood in *The Color
                    Purple*," *Modern Fiction Studies,* vol.
                    34, no. 1, 1988.

Lindsey Tucker   "Alice Walker's *The Color Purple*:
                    Emergent Woman, Emergent Text,"
                    Black American Literature Forum, vol.
                    11, no. 1, 1988.

Internet Sources

Jamie Gumbrecht   "Race, Ethnicity Can Be Challenge to
                   Gay Acceptance," *CNN,* 2010.
                   www.cnn.com.

Scott Simon   "50 Years Later, 'Mockingbird'
               Remains Relevant," Interview with
               James McBride, National Public
               Radio, July 10, 2010. www.npr.org.

Index

A

Abel, Elizabeth, 73
Abortion, 21
Abuse
    sexual, 53
    of women, 9–10, 22–23, 41–
        42, 98–104, 130–133
Africa, sexism in, 23, 45–46, 70–71
African American folk culture,
    91–93
African American history, 17
African American oral culture,
    79–80
African Americans. *See* Black
    men; Black women
Albert (*Color Purple*)
    Celie and, 53, 63, 71, 102–106
    Shug and, 43, 67, 71
    slavery and, 66
    transformation of, 40–41, 48,
        104–106, 109
Alcohol abuse, 10
Alphonso (*Color Purple*), 53, 54,
    92, 99–102
Angelou, Maya, 33
Audience identification, 83–85
Awards, 9

B

Babb, Valerie, 74–80
Baldwin, James, 122
Bambara, Toni Cade, 89–91
Ban Ki-moon, 131
*Beauty: When the Other Dancer Is
    the Self* (Walker), 24–25, 27

Bell, Bernard, 48
Beloved (Morrison), 32
Berlant, Lauren, 33
Bird imagery, 60–62
Black community
    sexism in, 21, 48–49
    stereotypes of, 118–119
    of Walker's childhood, 19
Black empowerment, 136
Black feminism, 22–23, 33–35,
    134–140
Black men
    abuse of black women by, 10
    portrayed in *The Color Purple*,
        81–83, 98–109, 120–121
    response of, to *The Color
        Purple*, 48–49, 84–85, 120–
        121
    stereotypes of, 118–119
    Walker and, 81–88
Black women
    abuse of, 9–11, 22–23
    blues singers, 34–35
    businesses started by, 11
    double burden of, 10, 17
    feminist ideologies of, 134–
        140
    mission of, 85–86
    oppression of, 86
    oral tradition and, 74–80
    parallels between African and
        Southern, 44–46, 70–71
    portrayed in *The Color Purple*,
        113–123
    rape of, in literature, 59–63
    reaction of, to *The Color
        Purple*, 82, 114–116
    resistance by, 94–95

sexism experienced by, 23
stereotypes of, 9
suppression of, 66–67
Walker on, 85–86
in white society, 11, 17
women's movement and, 86
writers, 21–22, 75–76
Block, Susan, 132
Blood imagery, 60–62
Blues music, 34–36, 93
The Bluest Eye (Morrison), 59, 60
Bol, Marsha, 126
Bradley, David, 81, 86, 87
Byerman, Keith E., 89–97

C

Cannon, Katie Geneva, 136
Celie (*Color Purple*)
    Albert and, 53, 63, 71, 102–106
    business of, 73, 96, 109–110
    emotional state of, 52–53
    fairy-tale elements of, 91
    feelings of, toward men, 41
    God and, 40–45, 49, 63, 68–69, 76–79, 92, 102, 104
    Harpo and, 93, 103
    impact of lack of mother on, 50–57
    inspiration for, 23, 66
    letters of, 33–34, 42, 62–64, 69–70, 75–80
    marriage of, 53, 102–104
    mistreatment of, 39–42, 53, 100–104
    Nettie and, 40, 55
    peace for, 49
    rape of, 60, 62–63, 92, 100
    resistance by, 95

Shug and, 35–36, 42–43, 47, 51–52, 56, 68–71, 95–96, 103–104
    Sofia and, 93–94, 103
    submissiveness of, 67–68, 119–120
    transformation of, 36, 62–63, 68–70, 98–107, 109–110
    Whoopi Goldberg as, *116*
    writing by, 92–93
Cheque Oitedie Cooperative, 128
Childhood trauma, 36–37
Chodorow, Nancy, 73
Christian, Barbara T., 16–23
Cisse, Aissata, 130–131
Civil rights movement, 20, 83
Cleage, Pearl, 137, 139
Clitoridectomy, 45, 70
Collins, Patricia Hill, 134–140
The Color Purple (Walker)
    audience for, 84–85
    awards won by, 9
    closure in, 96–97, 110–111
    contradictions in, 32–33
    critical responses to, 9, 31–32, 50–51, 82–83
    as disservice to black women, 113–123
    as fairy tale, 91–92, 96, 121–122
    female oppression in, 39–49
    feminist context of, 33–35
    film adaptation, 9, *52, 76, 101*
    folktale elements in, 91–93
    gender roles in, 46–47, 65–73
    imagery in, 60–62
    issues addressed in, 11, 22–23
    moral failure of, 117
    oral tradition and, 74–80
    portrayal of men in, 47–48, 81–83, 98–109, 120–121
    setting of, 33

stereotypes in, 117–119
writing of, 22
Constable, Anne, 125–129
Cutter, Martha J., 58–64

D

Daly, Mary, 45
DeGeneres, Ellen, 141–142
Dixon, Henry O., 98–107
Domestic violence, 130–133

E

Economic status, in black households, 11

F

Fairy tales, 91–92, 96, 121–122
Family networks, 72–73
Fanon, Frantz, 84
Fantasy, 111–112
Father
rape of Celie by her, 60, 62–
63, 92, 100
relationship between Walker
and her, 87–88
Female bonding, 51–52, 55–56,
70–73
Female genital mutilation, 45, 70
Female sexuality, 42–43
Feminism, 22–23, 33–35, 134–140
Film adaptation, 9, *52, 76, 101*
Folk art, 89–97, 125–129
Folk wisdom, 92
Froula, Christine, 33–34

G

García Márquez, Gabriel, 112
Gates, Henry Louis, 35
Gay rights, 142–145

Gender inequality, 133
Gender roles, 40–41, 45–47, 65–73
God
Celie's relationship with, 40–
45, 78–79, 102, 104
Celie's writing to, 63, 76–77,
92
genderless, 43–44
Shug and, 48, 68–69
Goldberg, Whoopi, 9, *116*
Gonzales, Ramona, 133
Griffin, Susan, 59–60

H

Hall, David, 145
Happiness, 111
Harpo (*Color Purple*)
Albert and, 47–48, 71, 73
Celie and, 93, 103
manhood of, 121
Sofia and, 46–47, 67, 94
Harris, Trudier, 57, 82, 113–123
Henderson, Mae G., 65
His Eye Is on the Sparrow
(Waters), 35–37
Historical novels, 33
Homosexuality, 141–150
hooks, bell, 108–112
Hurston, Zora Neale, 33, 35, 36,
95

I

I Know Why the Caged Bird Sings
(Angelou), 33, 111
In Love and Trouble (Walker), 21
In Search of Our Mothers' Gardens
(Walker), 24
Incest, 23, 53, 54, 63

J

Jacob, Harriet Ann, 119
James, John Angell, 10

K

Karpel, Ari, 141–150
Kate (*Color Purple*), 55–56
King, Coretta, 85–86
Kors, Geoff, 144–145

L

Language
    power of, 70
    as tool, 64
Lauret, Maria, 31–37
Lesbian relationships, 47, 104,
    141–150
Literacy, 70, 75–78
Lolosoli, Rebecca, 125–126
Louis-Dreyfus, Julia, 142, 150
Lucibello, Wanda, 132–133
Lynchings, 18

M

Male domination, 75–78, 92, 100–
    102, 109
Materialism, 109
Men
    alcohol abuse by, 10
    Celie's feelings toward, 41
    cruelty by, 98–107
    portrayed in *The Color Purple*,
        47–48, 108–109
    reaction of, to *The Color
        Purple*, 81–82
    Walker's view of, 86–88
    See also Black men
Metamorphoses (Ovid), 60

Miner, Madonne, 59
Mister. *See* Albert (*Color Purple*)
Morality, 117, 118
Morrison, Toni, 32, 59, 60
Mother-daughter bond, 50–57
Mr. ———. *See* Albert (*Color
    Purple*)
Murray, Pauli, 139

N

Naylor, Gloria, 59
Nettie (*Color Purple*), 40
    Celie and, 55
    letters of, 43–45, 54, 69–70,
        75–77, 79–80
    life in Africa for, 45, 70
    loss of mother for, 56–57
    sexism experienced by, 23
Nineteen Fifty-Five (Walker), 35
Nkubana, Janet, 129

O

OckPopTok, 128
Omolade, Barbara, 134
Once (Walker), 16, 21
Oral tradition, 74–80
Ovid, 60

P

Patriarchy, 9–10, 67–68, 109
Philomela, 58–64, *61*
Pinckney, Darryl, 33
Pluralism, 136
Proposition 8, 142, 146–147
Proudfit, Charles L., 50–57
Pulitzer Prize, 9

Q

Quilting, 93–94

R

Racial stereotypes, 117–119
Racism, 18, 21, 23, 48
Rape, 58–64, 80, 92, 100
Reid, Doris, 27, 29
Rock, Chris, 149–150
Royster, Philip M., 81–88
Rwanda, 128–129

S

Same-sex marriage, 146–147
Santa Fe International Folk Art
  Market, *127*
Sarah Lawrence College, 20–21
Saussure, Ferdinand de, 80
Seriff, Suzanne, 126–128
Sex roles, 40–41, 45–47, 65–73
Sexism
    in Africa, 45–46
    in black community, 21,
      48–49
    in *The Color Purple*, 48–49
    violence and, 23
Sexual abuse, 53
Sexual orientation, 141–150
Sexual themes, 22–23
Shame, 92–93
Shange, Ntozake, 49
Shug (*Color Purple*)
    Albert and, 43, 67, 71
    Celie and, 35–36, 42–43, 47,
      51–52, 56, 68–71, 95–96,
      103–104
    as folk figure, 95–96
    God and, 44, 68–69

inspiration for, 35
    masculinity of, 47, 71–72
    occupation of, 35
Slavery, 66–67
Smith, Mamie, *34*, 35
Smith, Nadine, 150
Social change, through folk art,
  125–129
Sofia (*Color Purple*)
    Celie and, 40, 93–94, 103
    Harpo and, 46–47, 67
    misfortunes of, 110
South
    racism in, 18
    sexism in, 45, 70–71
Spearman, Doug, 147–148
Spelman College, 18, 19–20
Spielberg, Steven, 40–41
Spirituality, 17, 109–111
Steinem, Gloria, 116, 117
Stereotypes, 9, 117–119
Sykes, Wanda, 141–150, *143*
Symbolism, 60–62

T

Temperance movement, 10
Their Eyes Were Watching God
  (Hurston), 36
The Third Life of Grange Copeland
  (Walker), 18, 21
Toomer, Jean, 120
Truth, Sojourner, 138

U

Umoja Uaso, Kenya, 125–126

V

Violence
    domestic, 130–133

against women, 9–10, 22–23, 41–42, 98–104

W

Walker, Alice
  audience and, 84–85
  black men and, 81–88
  childhood of, 17–19, 24–30
  college years for, 19–21
  eye injury of, 24–30, 87
  influences on, 35–37
  issues addressed in writings of, 16–17, 90–91
  photo of, 20
  relationship with father of, 87–88
  role of writer and, 83–84
Walker, Bobby, 26–27
Walker, Curtis, 25–27
Waters, Ethel, 35–36
Weakley, Sonya, 130–133
White, Evelyn C., 24–30
White domination, 75–78
White women, reaction to *The Color Purple* of, 116
Wife-beating, 10
Williams, Sherley, 136

Winchell, Donna Haisty, 39–49
Winfrey, Oprah, 9
Womanism, 22–23, 35, 135–137, 140
Women
  abuse of, 9–10, 22–23, 41–42, 98–104, 130–133
  in Africa, 45–46, 70–71
  love between, 42–43
  oral tradition and, 74–80
  social definition of, 21
The Women of Brewster Place (Naylor), 59
Women's movement, 10, 83, 86
Writer
  as alienated rescuer, 83
  audience and, 83–85
Writing
  act of, 75–76
  shame and, 92–93
  as tool of domination, 76–78
  transformation of, 80

Y

You Can't Keep a Good Woman Down (Walker), 34–35